Eastern Naturalist In The West

DALLAS LORE SHARP, 1912

[signature]

2005

SAND
LAKE
PRESS

ABOUT THE EDITOR

Worth Mathewson is the author of ten books about birds, nature and stories we love to read about those special times spent outdoors. He has written avian articles for *National Geographic*, *Audubon*, *Natural History*, *International Wildlife*, *Birder's World*, and *Bird Watcher's Digest*.

He and his wife, Margaret Thompson Mathewson, live on a 20 acre farm in Western Oregon.

Eastern Naturalist In The West

DALLAS LORE SHARP, 1912

Where Rolls The Oregon, by Dallas Lore Sharp, was first published
by Houghton Mifflin Company in 1914.

Copyright 2001

ISBN 0-9711872-0-7
Printed in Canada

Library of Congress Card Catalog Number 2001 131846

Address all inquiries to:
SAND LAKE PRESS
PO Box 130
Amity, Oregon 97101
(503)843-2767

Book Design by Lydia Inglett Spears

Contents

Acknowledgements

I read *Where Rolls the Oregon* **nearly fifty years ago.** Prior to this I was already intently interested in the work of William Finley. As a very young child the Finley/Bohlman photographs in my first book of birds, *Birds of America*, published in 1917, edited by the great T. Gilbert Pearson, with color art by Louis Agassiz Fuertes, never failed to catch my attention. I can recall with clarity my amazement as a five-year-old with the full page photograph on page 26. It pictured Finley and Bohlman climbing a sheer rock cliff in order to reach a colony of nesting murres.

Today I have a poster size enlargement of this photograph in our front hall. I've had it for over twenty years, and still frequently pause to enjoy it.

Where Rolls The Oregon acted as a catalyst for me to begin serious research into the life and work of William Finley. Through Dallas Lore Sharp's account of his summer of 1912 in Oregon with Finley, I was able to have a first hand account of time spent in the field with the man in whom I had developed a strong, early interest. In 1986, years of research helped me write my book, *William L. Finley, Pioneer Wildlife Photographer*, with a foreword by Roger Tory Peterson.

Since that time it has proven to be enjoyable to spend time researching the life of Dallas Lore Sharp, and provide present day readers with an edited version of his summer with Finley. In doing so, I want to thank Mr. Charles Niles, Special Collections, Mugar Memorial Library, Boston University, for his interest and aid in the letters Dallas Lore sharp wrote to his wife, Grace, while traveling with the Finley party.

Thanks also to the late Captain Ted Bohlman for the gift of many old photographs and glass negatives from his father's collection.

Thanks to the many people who have read *Where Rolls The*

Oregon at my request, and provided valuable opinions as to reprinting the book.

Thanks also to the Oregon Historical Society for making photographs available from their Finley collection. These are listed by chapter. Cover photograph: OHS # 823. Chapter II: OHS # 807 and 2519. Chapter III: OHS # 2523. Chapter IV: # 839 and 845. Chapter VII: OHS # 1604 and 182. Chapter VIII: OHS: # 399, 317 and 360. Chapter IX: OHS: # JRD. Chapter X: OHS # 609. Chapter XI: OHS # 864.

—Worth Mathewson

Amity, Oregon, May 2001

Preface

It was not to write a book that I visited the Northwest. One need not go so far from Massachusetts to do that. The apple trees under Mullein Hill are as full of books as

...the continuous woods
Where rolls the Oregon.

I spent the summer of 1912 in Oregon, studying the wild life of the State, the fish and game, and particularly the work of the Game Warden in its educational aspects. I took no pencil with me for fear I might write out my eyes. And Nature hates an interviewer anyway. So this volume is not a series of notes, but a group of impressions, deep, indelible impressions of the vast outdoors of Oregon.

"Vast" is the right word for Oregon, vast and varied—the most alluring land to the naturalist within the compass of our coasts. From Three Arch Rocks in the Pacific to the broad backs of the Steens we traveled; from the peaks of the Wallowas to the tule marshes of Klamath Lake Reservation—a summer far greater than the pages of this book. For I have not spoken of the firs of the Coast Range, nor of the pines of the Cascades, nor of the orchards of the river valleys, nor of the salmon of the Columbia, nor of a hundred other things that together give character and personality to the State. Nor have I spoken of the hospitality of the people; space would fail me, for it is the largest thing in the State.

But here I must thank Mr. William Lovell Finley, the State Game Warden, to whom I owe my summer in Oregon; and here express my keen appreciation of the great work he is doing. To his friend, and my friend, Herman T. Bohlman, I am also deeply indebted; as well as to the deputy wardens who were extraordinarily kind and helpful to me.

Oregon, and the country as a whole, owe Finley and Bohlman a large debt for what they have done to preserve wild life. It was largely due to their efforts that the great Federal reservations of Oregon were set aside.

I wish to thank them and Mr. George M. Weister of Portland, for the use of their splendid photographs as illustrations for this book. My thanks are due also to the Editors of the *Atlantic Monthly*, *Country Life In America*, and *St. Nicholas* for privilege to reprint the chapters that appeared first in their magazines.

—Dallas Lore Sharp
Mullein Hill, May 1914

Chapter I Westward

My dear Mr Sharp,

Now don't be governed too much by the suggestions and demands of your publishers. They will want to crowd you to death not because they have your own interest at heart but because they think they can make a little on the sale of books. Let Century Co. wait a year. Don't be too anxious to listen to them. They will be after you harder if you just put them off one year and they will be willing to pay more. Keep your prices high, set them and they will come to you.

You need this Oregon trip. It will open your eyes and put new blood in your veins. Not that your eyes are shut but there are lots of things out here you need to see. You are working for the future and you need new material and you can get it here. Your roots are getting too cramped in that barren New England soil. You may stay right there, if you listen to your publishers, and turn out several more books; but they will be worth more to you and the public if you will take a good vacation and write a book a year later.

We want you to bundle up all the boys and come out West with Mrs. Sharp. I've got a position for you at ninety dollars a month and all your traveling expenses paid, you will not have much to do either except go with me around the state. Let me know when you are coming. If you can't put the publishers off, go to a doctor and get him to prove your health is failing and you must have a complete change of rest, he can prescribe two months in the high altitude of eastern Oregon.

Mrs. F. joins me in best wishes to you and yours.

Sincerely,
William L. Finley, April 13, 1912.

When **Dallas Lore Sharp traveled** with his family from Hingham, Massachusetts to Jennings Lodge, Oregon, up river from Portland, and were greeted warmly by William and Irene Finley, two of North America's best known nature writers united for a memorable summer. It was the summer of 1912, ultimately the foundation for several *Atlantic Monthly* magazine articles by Sharp the following year, and the book *Where Rolls The Oregon* published by Houghton Mifflin Company in 1914.

During the decade preceding the summer, both men had rapidly become familiar names to the reading public. Dallas Lore Sharp was a college professor, magazine writer, and was best known for books which sold extremely well.

New Jersey historian and writer, Frank Bertolini, has worked extensively with Sharp research. His efforts have added much to our insight into the man. From Bertolini's studies we find that Sharp was born on December 13, 1870 in Haleyville, N.J. While in high school Sharp became friends with an elderly naturalist who was curator for the Brown University museum. Sharp was hired as a collector for the south New Jersey region.

In 1891 Sharp entered Brown University. He excelled in numerous areas: he worked at the museum as an assistant, was a sports reporter for the college, was editor of the school's literary magazine, and was on the track team as a distance runner, setting a world's record for the two mile run.

After graduation he married Grace Hastings and was ordained as a Methodist preacher. He re-entered a university—this time Boston University—to complete theological school. While serving as a pastor in the area he also became a librarian at the college and in 1899 began teaching English. In 1900 he became a staff member of the popular magazine *Youth Companion*. In 1901 he wrote the first of his many books, *Wild Life Near Home*. The book was illustrated by Bruce Horsfall, who went on to become one of America's most noted wildlife illustrators.

Within just a decade Sharp was known as one of the most popular writers and speakers of the era. He frequently gave lectures from coast to coast. Books such as his 1903 *A Watcher in the Woods* sold over 100,000 copies. With his success, Sharp briefly became interested in politics and ran for a U.S. Senate seat from Massachusetts against Henry Cabot Lodge. Sharp lost the election, but just barely.

At the height of his career Dallas Lore Sharp was considered on a par with Henry David Thoreau, John Burroughs, John Muir,

William Finley with bird skin, 1896

Bradford Torrey, and Olive Thorne Miller, all superb nature writers. During President Theodore Roosevelt's term, Sharp was invited to the White House. He and his wife had a country home at Mullein Hill in Hingham, Massachusetts. They had four sons. On November 29, 1929, Sharp passed away from a brain tumor at the age of 59.

William Lovell Finley was born in Santa Clara, California, on August 9, 1876. He died on June 29, 1953. In 1887 John Finley moved to Portland, Oregon, and William made friends with the boy next door, Herman Bohlman. It was to be a lifelong and important friendship. Young William Finley had been interested in birds since early childhood. He introduced Herman Bohlman to ornithology and sparked a similar strong interest. By 1894 Finley and Bohlman helped form the North-Western Ornithological Association. This group increased to twenty-two members by 1896 with young Finley as president. Most of the group's activities were based on collecting eggs and skins of birds.

In 1897 Finley and Bohlman began photographing wildlife. Both

Herman Bohlman with camera

had cameras. But soon the pair entered into a partnership which saw Bohlman do most, but not all, of the photography, and Finley did the writing of articles based around the photos. In the spring of 1900 they photographed a red-tailed hawk's nest from eggs to fledging young. Finley sold an article along with the photographs, and within the next eight years the team of Finley/Bohlman produced a staggering number of photographs and articles. Like Dallas Lore Sharp, William Finley rose to national prominence in less than a decade.

Some of the work done by Finley and Bohlman, such as the California Condor project in 1906, where they photographed a condor just minutes out of the egg to the point when it fledged, was both remarkable and important. Their skill and pioneering wildlife photographs established benchmarks for others to follow.

William Finley had entered the University of California in 1899. His work with Bohlman was done during summer vacations or when Bohlman traveled down to California. He graduated in 1903, and like Sharp, taught English at the university level. In 1906 Finley married Nellie Irene Barnhart, and they moved back to Portland, Oregon. They built a small house on ten acres on the banks of the Willamette River at Jennings Lodge near Portland. They had two children, William Jr. and Phoebe Katherine.

While both Dallas Lore Sharp and William Finley rapidly reached pinnacles of popularity and recognition, their personalities and temperament differed. Sharp was philosophical and highly literate. Finley was aggressively dynamic and frequently blunt.

Early in his career William Finley became an environmental activist, and remained so for his entire life. He was a leader and a doer. Thus, not only did he and Bohlman produce a lot of important photographs, and Finley articles were widely published in many magazines, William Finley was in the center of efforts for wildlife and the environment. He always viewed these efforts as the most important of all he did.

During the rebirth of the Audubon Society in the early 1900s, Finley was a ground floor supporter. Nearly all of this early Audubon Society movement was based on the East coast. Out in the West, Finley was almost the sole voice. He was appointed a Field

Window display of Finley's first book, 1907

Naturalist for the Society, then helped form the Oregon Audubon Society, and was elected President.

Of all of William Finley's efforts, none were more important than his farsighted establishment of wildlife refuges. Finley's chief ally with refuges was Theodore Roosevelt, who viewed Finley as a great favorite and personal friend. Finley, for example, traveled back to New York to teach Kermit Roosevelt the use of a camera in wildlife photography prior to the Roosevelt safari to Africa in 1910.

During Roosevelt's Presidency he created many refuges, including three very important ones in Oregon due to Finley's urging. The trio were Three Arch Rocks in 1907—the first refuge in the West—and the vast Malheur and Klamath refuges in 1908. During the last years of his life William Finley viewed these refuges as his greatest accomplishment.

In 1910 Governor Oswall West asked Finley to create a Department of Fish & Game for the state. In 1912 West appointed

Finley State Game Warden, which made him head of the Department. It was in this capacity that Finley invited Dallas Lore Sharp to Oregon for the summer of 1912.

Finley made plans to take Sharp over Oregon, including those places where he and Bohlman had done much of their early work, such as Three Arch Rocks in 1903, Klamath marshes in 1905, and Malheur marsh in 1908. He asked Bohlman to join them, and he agreed. Herman Bohlman had entered his father's plumbing business in 1899, married Maud Bittleston in 1908, and had greatly curtailed his photography from that point. The Finley/Bohlman 1908 Malheur trip marked the last time the men worked together on a large project. For the 1912 Sharp visit Bohlman took the summer off to help. During the trip Bohlman used a still camera. Finley was deeply involved in making movies by that time and he used a motion picture camera.

Sharp arrived in Oregon in June with his family. His wife and three of the children stayed with Irene at Jennings Lodge, while on several trips, Sharp and his oldest son, Dallas Jr., traveled with the Finley party. The summer was done in segments, with a return to Jennings Lodge briefly before setting out again. Members accompanying Finley and Sharp varied on the different trips, but included Herman Bohlman, and Stanley Jewett (later co-author with Ira Gabrielson of *Birds of Oregon*).

As the party made their way around the state, Sharp wrote to his wife back at Jennings Lodge. Unfortunately only a few of the letters remain, but those which do, from the special collections at Boston College, are reproduced here. These letters give an interesting insight into Sharp's shaping of the book of his 1912 summer in Oregon, *Where Rolls The Oregon*. And in his graceful, sometimes flowery style, he captures the wildness and vastness of Oregon just after the turn of the century.

In this reprinting of *Where Rolls The Oregon* under the new title of *Eastern Naturalist In The West: Dallas Lore Sharp, 1912*, the editor needs to point out that portions of Sharp's writings were omitted. Also the chapters were rearranged. During consideration of reprinting Where Rolls The Oregon, several individuals were requested to make their evaluation of the book's interest to present day readers.

All suggested that while the book was a treasure trove of important wildlife history, Sharp's at times leaving the subject at hand for several pages in a rambling, intellectual exploration, detracted from the enjoyment of the read. Therefore, portions were removed. In fairness, one reviewer felt the book should be reprinted intact even though he admitted to having problems with parts.

Another reviewer posed the question of how and when Sharp and Finley met. This appears lost to history, but the editor would strongly suspect that the meeting took place between 1903 and 1905 when Finley made trips to the East to speak of his western bird and wildlife work. For almost certain they met, or saw one another again, in 1907 after Charles Scribner's Sons published William Finley's *American Birds*. Scribner's arranged a large speaking and book signing tour for Finley, which included Boston, Sharp's home.

The same reviewer questioned how well the book sold, and what was Finley's reaction. Sharp's publisher, Houghton Mifflin Company, could supply no sales records, but suggested that all of Sharp's books enjoyed large sales. As for Finley's reaction, the editor recalls reading a letter written by Finley a few years after the book was published which led the editor to believe that Finley was amused by portions of Sharp's digressions away from the subject.

For those interested in the unedited *Where Rolls The Oregon*, old copies can be found without difficulty. Powell's City of Books in Portland, Oregon, seemingly always has copies available. Likewise, many libraries in the Pacific Northwest have copies which would be readily accessible via interlibrary loan.

In any event, Sharp's writings of his summer of 1912 in Oregon certainly stand up well to the aging process, and now provide us, especially those of us who have spent time in the locations he writes of, with a powerful, at times emotional, insight into our priceless natural heritage.

—Worth Mathewson
Amity, Oregon, 2001

Chapter 11 Three Arch Rocks

Three Arch Rocks are three jagged basalt formations several hundred yards off shore on the north Oregon coast. These great rocks lie just south of the entrance to Tillamook Bay, and directly in front of the hamlet of Oceanside. In the spring and early summer they are nesting grounds for thousands of common murre, pigeon guillemot, tufted puffin, Brandt's cormorant, forked-tailed and Beal's petrels, and western gull. In 1901 Finley and Bohlman, along with Ron Nicholas and Ellis Hadley, made a collecting and photography trip to Three Arch Rocks. But weather prevented them from staying out on the rocks more than just a few hours.

In 1903 Finley and Bohlman returned by themselves. They were forced to camp on the beach for 16 days before the seas calmed enough to allow them to launch a boat into the surf. Once out to the rocks they used a block and tackle to pull the boat up on a ledge. They camped on this ledge for nearly a week and obtained a series of excellent photographs. After viewing these photographs, President Roosevelt decreed the rocks as a Federal Bird Refuge.

Much like the Finley/Bohlman 1901 attempt, Sharp's 1912 stay on Three Arch Rocks was brief because of weather. But they did spend the night, sleeping on the ledge in the rain. And they did make the dangerous climb to the top of Shag Rock, the outer-most of the three. With them was Sharp's eleven year old son.

The fog was lifting. The thick, wet drift that had threatened us on Tillamook Bar stood clear of the shouldering sea to the westward, and in toward shore, like an upper sea, hung at the fir-girt middles of the mountains, as level and as gray as the sea below. There was now no breeze. The long, smooth swell of the Pacific swung under us and in, until it whitened at the base of three dark rocks that lay in our course, and which now began to take on form out of the foggy distance. Gulls were flying over us; lines of black cormorants and crowds of murres were winging past toward the rocks; but we were still too far away from the looming piles to see that the gray of their walls was the gray of uncounted colonies of nesting birds, colonies that covered the craggy steeps as the green firs clothed the slopes of the Coast Range mountains, up to the hanging fog.

As we steamed on nearer, the sound of the surf about the rocks became audible; the birds in the air grew more numerous, their cries now faintly mingling with the sound of the sea. The hole in the Middle Rock, a mere fleck of foam at first, widened rapidly into an arching tunnel through which our boat might have run; the sea began to break before us over half-sunken ledges; and soon upon us fell the damp shadows of Three-Arch Rocks, for now we were looking far up at their sides, at the sea-birds in their guano-gray rookeries—gulls, cormorants, guillemots, puffins, murres—encrusting the ragged walls from tide-line to pinnacle, as the crowding barnacles encrusted the bases from the tide-line down.

We were not approaching without protest, for the birds were coming off to meet us, more and more the nearer we drew, wheeling and clacking overhead in a constantly thickening cloud of lowering wings and tongues. We rounded the outer, Shag Rock, and headed slowly in toward the yawning hole of Middle Rock as into some mighty cave, so sheer and shadowy rose the walls above us, so like to cavern thunder was the throbbing of the surf through the hollow arches, was the flapping and screaming of the birds against the high circling walls, was the deep menacing grumble of the lions, as though the muffle of surf and sea-fowl, herd after herd lumbered bellowing into the foam.

It was a strange, wild scene. Hardly a mile from the Oregon coast, but cut off by breaker and bar from the abrupt, uninhabited shore, the three rocks of the Reservation, each pierced with its resounding arch, heaved their heavy shoulders from the waves straight up, huge, towering, till our little steamer coasted their dripping sides like some puffing pigmy. They were sea rocks, of no part or lot with the dry land, their beryl basins wave-scooped, and set with purple starfish, with green and pink anemones, and beaded many deep with mussels of amethyst and jet, a glitter in the water's overflow; and just above the jeweled basins, like fabled beasts of old, lay the sea-lions, lumpish, uncouth forms, flippered, reversed in shape, with throats like the caves of Aeolus, hollow, hoarse, discor-

Finley and Bohlman on Three Arch Rocks

dant; and higher up, on every jutting bench and shelf, in every weathered rift, over every jog of the ragged cliffs, to their bladed backs and pointed peaks, swarmed the sea-birds, web-footed, amphibious, wave-shaped, with stormy voices given them by the winds that sweep in from the sea. And their numbers were the numbers of the sea.

Crude, crowded, weltering, such life could never have been brought forth and nurtured by the dry land; her breasts had withered at the birth. Only the bowels of the wide, wet sea could breed these heaps, these cones of life that rose volcanic from the waves, their craters clouded by the smoke of wings, their belted bases rumbling with a multi-throated thunder. The air was dank with the must of a closed room—closed for an aeon past—no breath of the land, no odor of herb, no scent of fresh soil; but the raw, rank smell of rookery and den, saline, kelpy, fetid; the stench of fish and bedded guano; and pools of reeking ammonia where the lion herds lay sleeping on the lower rocks in the sun.

A boat's keel was beneath me, but as I stood out on the pointed prow, barely above the water, and found myself thrust forward without will or effort among the crags and caverns, among the shadowy walls, the damps, the smells, the sounds; among the bellowing beasts in the churning waters about me, and into the storm of wings and tongues in the whirring air above me, I passed from the things I had known, and the time and the earth of man, into a period of the past, elemental, primordial, monstrous.

I had not known what to expect, because, never having seen Three-Arch Rocks, I could not know what my friend the State Game Warden meant when he said to me, "Come out to the Pacific Coast, and I will take you back to your cave days; I will show you life as it was lived at the beginning of the world." I had left my Hingham garden with its woodchuck, for the coast of Oregon, a journey that might have been compassed by steam, that might have been measured in mere miles, had it stopped short of Three-Arch Rocks Reservation, which lay seaward just off the shore. Instead of miles, it was zones, ages, worlds that were traveled as I passed into this haunt of wild sea-bird and beast. And I found myself saying over to myself, "Thou madest him to have dominion over the works of thy hands;

thou hast put all things under his feet"—as if words had never before been uttered in human ears, and could not yet be understood.

For here was no man-dominion; here the trampling feet of man had never passed. Here was the primeval world, the fresh and unaffrighted morning of the Fifth Day. Then as the brute in me shook itself and growled back at the brute about me, something touched my arm, and I turned to find the Federal Warden of the Rocks at my side—God, as it were, seeing again everything that He had made, everything that man had unmade, and saying again with a new and a larger meaning, Have dominion over the fowl of the air, and over the fish of the sea, and over whatsoever passeth through the paths of the seas.

And here at my side, by act of Congress, stood that Dominion, the Federal Warden, the collective, spiritual man, badged and armed to protect forever against the individual brute man the wild life of these three rocks and the waters adjacent.

But did I fully understand the Why? Did I wholly comprehend the meaning and the value of such a sanctuary for wild life? I turned to the warden with the question. That honest official paused a moment, then slowly answered that he'd be hanged if he knew why. He didn't see any good in such protection; his salary notwithstanding. He had caught a cormorant (one from the Rocks) not long since, that had forty-nine young salmon in its maw; and for the sea-lions, they were an unmitigated nuisance, each one of them destroying (so it had been reckoned) five hundred pounds of fish every day.

Now the warden's findings are open to question, because there are good reasons for the cormorant's catch being other than salmon fry; and as for the lions it is pretty certain that during their stay on the breeding-grounds (Three-Arch Rocks) they do not feed at all, having come in from their deep-sea wanderings with fat enough to worry along with until their family cares are over. A bull sea-lion with half a dozen wives has his flippers full. They come in to the Rocks fat; they depart lean; and when afar on the waves the chances are few that salmon ever become their prey. Still I have no proof of error in the warden's figures. I will accept them just now—the five hundred pounds of fish a day for the sea-lion, and the forty-nine salmon fry for the cormorant (they would easily total, four years later, on their way up the Columbia to the canneries, a half ton)—accepting this fearful loss of Chinook salmon then as real, is there any answer to my question, Why? Any good and sufficient reason for setting aside such a reservation as Three-Arch Rocks? For myself protecting the wild life of these barren rocks against myself?

No, perhaps not—not if this protection of cormorants and sea-lions means the utter loss of the salmon as an industry and as an article of food. But there is an adequate and a paying catch of salmon being taken in the Columbia this year, in spite of the lions and the cormorants, as there will be again next year, for the state hatcheries have liberated over seven million young salmon this summer and sent them safely down the Columbia to the sea. No, perhaps not—no good and sufficient reason for such protection, were I an Astoria fisherman with the sea-lions pursuing the salmon into my nets, as the imaginative fishermen say they occasionally do. Instead of an Astoria fisherman, I am a teacher of literature in Boston on the other side of the world. It is easy at Boston to believe in the value of Astoria sea-lions. It is hard anywhere not to believe in canned salmon. Yet, as sure as the sun shines, and the moon, there are some things utterly without an equivalent in canned salmon.

Among these things are Three-Arch Rocks and Malheur Lake and Klamath Lake Reservations in Oregon, and the scores of other bird and animal preserves created by Congress all the way from the coast of Maine across the States and overseas to the Hawaiian Islands. They were set aside only yesterday; the sportsman, the pelt-hunter, the plume-hunter, the pot-hunter, and in some instances the legitimate fisherman and farmer ordered off to make room for the beast and the bird. Small wonder if there is some grumbling, some law-breaking, some failure to understand. But that will pass.

These were Isles of Life. Here, in the rocky caverns, was conceived and brought forth a life as crude and raw and elemental as the rock itself. It covered every crag. I clutched it in my hands; I crushed it under my feet; it was thick in the air about me. My narrow path up the face of the rock was a succession of sea-bird rookeries, of crowded eggs, and huddled young, hairy or naked or wet from the shell. Every time my fingers felt for a crack overhead, they touched some-

Sharp and son with Bohlman on Three Arch Rocks

thing warm that rolled or squirmed; every time my feet moved under me for a hold, they pushed in among top-shaped eggs that turned on the shelf or went over far below; and whenever I hugged the pushing wall I must bear off from a mass of squealing, struggling, shapeless things, just hatched. And down upon me, as rookery after rookery of old birds whirred in fright from their ledges, fell crashing eggs and unfledged young, that the greedy gulls devoured ere they touched the sea.

An alarmed wing-beat, the excited turn of a webbed foot, and the murre's single egg or its single young was sent over the edge, so narrow was the footing for Life, so yawning the pit below. But up out the churning waters, up from crag to crag, clambers Life, by beak, by claw, falling, clinging, climbing, with the odds forever favoring Death, yet with Life forever finding wings.

I was midway in my climb, at a bad turn, edging inch by inch along, my face hard-pressed to the face of the cliff, my fingers grip-

Finley and Bohlman in camp on Three Arch Rocks

ping a slight seam overhead, my feet feeling blindly at the brink beneath, when there came up to me, small and smothered, the wash of the waves—the voice of space and nothingness and void, the call of the chasm out of which I was so hardly climbing. A cold hand clasped me from behind.

With an impulse as instinctive as the unfledged murre's, I flattened against the toppling rock, fingers and feet, elbows, knees, and chin clinging desperately to the narrow chance—a falling fragment of shale, a gust of wind, the wing-stroke of a frightened bird, enough to break my hold and swing me out over the water, washing faint and far below. A long breath, and I was climbing again.

Yet in that instant I was born again, not a human being, but a mere being; stripped of everything except life and the clinging to life; reduced to one of my moments of time through the aeons of my development back to the bird of me, back to my murre self, catching by chin, knees, elbows, feet, and fingers to the rocky seams for life, naked life. I was reborn a murre, fighting against the forces of sea and sky, to live, to cling to the rock from the wind and waves. And there was born within me that moment more life, more sympathy with life, a new consciousness of blood brotherhood with all birds and beasts and things that live.

We were on Shag Rock, our only possible ascent taking us up the sheer south face. With the exception of an occasional Western gull's and pigeon guillemot's nest, these steep sides were occupied entirely by the California murres—penguin-shaped birds about the size of a wild duck, chocolate-brown above, with white breasts, which literally covered the sides of the three great Rocks wherever they could find a hold. If a million meant anything, I should say there were a million murres nesting on this outer Rock; not nesting either, for the egg is laid upon the bare ledge, as you might place it upon a mantel, a single sharp-pointed egg, as large as a turkey's and just as many of them on the ledge as there is standing-room for the birds. The murre broods her egg by standing straight up over it, her short legs, by dint of stretching, allowing her to straddle the big egg, her short tail propping her securely from behind.

On up along the narrow back, or blade, of the Rock, and over the peak, were the well spaced nests of Brandt's cormorants, nests the size of an ordinary straw hat, made of sea-grass and the yellow-flowered sulphur-weed that grew in a dense mat over the north slope of the top, each nest holding four long, dirty, blue eggs or as many black, shivering young; and in the low sulphur-weed, all along the roof-like slope of the top, were the nests of the gulls and the burrows of the tufted puffins and the petrels. The cormorants were the most striking figures of the summit—all around the rock rim that dropped sheer to the sea they stood black, silent, statuesque. Everywhere were nests and eggs and young, and everywhere were flying, crying birds—above, about, and far below me, a whirling, whirring vortex of wings that had caught me in its funnel.

So thick was the air with wings, so clangorous with harsh tongues, that I had not seen the fog moving in, or noticed that the gray wind of Tillamook Bar had begun to growl about the crags. It was late, and the night that I had intended to spend on the summit would be dark and stormy, would be too wet and wild for watching, where one must hold on with one's hands so close to the edge, or slip and go over.

So we got over the rim along the south face of the cliff, up which we had climbed, and by rope descended to a small shelf under an overhanging ledge about forty feet above the waves. Here, protected from the northwest wind, and from much of the rain, we rolled up in our blankets, while night crept down upon us and out over the sea.

It was a gray, ghostly night of dusk and mist that swam round and round the crags and through the wakeful caverns in endless undulations, coiling its laving folds over the sunken ledges, and warping with slow, sucking sounds its mouthing tentacles round and through the rocks. Or was it only the wash of waves? Only the gray of the mist and the drip of the rain? Or was it the return of the waters? The resolving of firmament and rock back through the void of night into the flux of the sea?

It was a long night of small, distinct, yet multitudinous sounds. The confusion caused by our descent among the birds soon subsided; the large colony of murres close by our heads returned to their rookery; and with the rain and thickening dark there spread everywhere the quiet of a low murmurous quacking. Sleep was settling over the rookeries.

Down in the water below us rose the bulk of a sea-lion, an old lone bull, whose den we had invaded. He, too, was coming back to his bed for the night. He rose and sank in the half light, blinking dully at the cask and other things that we had left below us on the ledge belonging to him. Then he slowly clambered out and hitched up toward his bed. My own bed was just above his, so close that I could hear him blow, could see the scars on his small head, and a long open gash on his side. We were very near.

I drew back from the edge, pulled the blanket and sail-cloth over me, and turned my face up to the slanting rain. Two young gulls that had hidden from us in a cranny came down and nestled close to my head, their parents, one after the other, perching an instant on the rock just out of reach, and all through the night calling to them with a soft nasal quack to still their alarm. In the murre colony overhead there was a constant stir of feet and a soft, low talk; and over all the Rock, through all the darkened air, there was a silent coming and going of wings, shadow-wings of the petrel, some of them, that came winnowing in from afar on the sea.

The drizzle thickened; the night lengthened. Against my face lay the damp hair of my little son. He was sleeping soundly, the rhythm and rise of the tide in his deep, sweet breathing. The day of danger had brought him very close to me, so near that now I might almost have been the mother that bore him. The quiet deepened. I listened to the wings about me, to the murmur among the birds above me, to the stir of the sea beneath me, to the breathing of the sleeping men beside me, to the pulse of the life enfolding me, of which I was part and heart; and under my body I felt a narrow shelf of rock dividing the waters from the waters.

The drizzle thickened; the night lengthened; and—darkness was upon the face of the deep.

Chapter III   Mother Carey's Chickens

Sharp most hoped to see petrels while out on Three Arch Rocks. Due to the weather he wasn't able to wait by their burrows for their nocturnal activity. Had he been successful he would have seen the numerous Leach's petrel and perhaps the beautiful, less common forked-tailed petrel. Both species are a soft, sooty gray. They are small, somewhat under a martin in size, and adapted to their nocturnal habits in order to escape gulls, which, given the opportunity, can catch petrels in flight, and swallow them whole.

Had Sharp been able to wait in darkness for the petrel's activity he would have been rewarded, perhaps beyond his expectations. In large colonies, such as on Three Arch Rocks, the swarm of petrels around their burrows can be almost like bats around their cave. The petrel, and a petrel flight, is one of nature's true treasures.

"Up and down! Up and down!
From the base of the wave to the billow's crown,
And midst the flashing and feathery foam,
The stormy petrel finds a home."

Land had been lost since early morning. I don't remember how many miles we had made, but we had climbed far up the hill of the sea toward the second night, when across our bows cut a little band of small, dark birds with white rumps, which, veering, glancing down the ragged waves, seemed to settle in the wake of the ship. No one need be told that they were petrels—Mother Carey's chickens; but what I could hardly believe was that they were birds—with webbed feet, to be sure—but birds with wings, adrift here in the vast of the ocean, and with nests and mates waiting for them along some far-off rocky shore. They must have circled the ship, for soon again they came keeling across our bows into a curling wave-crest, and, riding down the trough, were on the wing and gone.

They went straight into the night and as if to meet the coming storm. For a keen wet wind was blowing. The decks were cleared and empty except for myself and the officer who leaned hard against the wind as he paced his watch. It was an inscrutable, fearful night into which I was faring. My feet were strange to the pitching deck; my spirit was not at home on the sea. But the birds—it was their path I was following—where in this wild night of waves and coming storm had they gone?

Down in the black water the porpoises were leaping. Off on the sea there was nothing, nothing but the closing circle of storm, and I was turning from the rail with a shiver, when, far out on the gray chop, I caught sight of the petrels, rising and falling with the heave and sag of the sea.

Did they sleep on the sea, I wonder? Not that night, perhaps, as this was the nesting season, but here night and day they pass the larger part of their lives. All through that long night I dreamed of them rising and falling on the chop. And often since, when the wind has been high, when the woods have roared and heaved, and the house has rocked in the might of the gale, I have seen that little brood of Mother Carey's chickens swirl through the breaking crest of some ghost wave, ride past my ship asleep, and vanish in the dream.

It is awesome enough to hear the creak of frozen branches, and the hiss of driving snow and rushing winds past your chamber, when you think that out in it all are the winter birds sleeping. They have a hundred shelters, however, a hundred hidings from the force of the storm. But on the unsheltered ocean there are only the yawning troughs that dip for a moment from the last of the winds, only the tossing tumult of the waves. Who could fail to ask, seeing this troop of birds far out on the ocean, Whence do they hail? And whither are they bound? Not much larger than swallows, they have dared all the great liner dares, and more. They have cleared from some shore, but the ocean is their home. They love the waves; they revel in the storm. If seen on the North Atlantic in the summer they may be our Leach's petrel that nest on the islands in the mouth of the Penobscot Bay and northward; or Wilson's petrel, a migrant from the south; or near the European coast, the little "stormy" petrel that breeds from the Shetland Islands to the Mediterranean.

There are certain birds that since my childhood have had a strong hold upon my imagination. One of these is the stormy petrel—all petrels being "stormy" to me. I cannot remember when his wide flung flight did not seem to me the very soul of the ocean, nor when I did not wish to follow him over the waves to his rookery on the cliffs. Yet I was a man before I saw my first flock of the birds skimming the waves of the Atlantic—a man in years, but still a child haunted by the lines of some poem called "The Stormy Petrel" read, or read to me, from some old McGuffey Reader, I imagine, before I ever started to school. A bird in a poem is worth almost as much to a child as a bird in a bush; perhaps more. I have learned many facts in the fields, but how many of my feelings have come to me out of books! I felt my stormy petrel long before I knew him. He was a poem long before he was a bird, and the beat of his wings must ever be—

> *"Up and down! Up and down!*
> *From the base of the wave to the billow's crown."*

I have not only seen him now, I have also followed him to his sea cliff and pulled him out of his tame little hole of a burrow. Here was his nest, where I might make mine. His nest, but this was not his home, for back come the lines—

> *"And midst the flashing and feathery foam,*
> *The stormy petrel finds a home."*

The poetry got in ahead of the ornithology. I am glad it did; for that is the happier order, I think; just as I am glad that we have our youth before our old age. One who is young first stands an excellent chance of never growing entirely old. And so with poems and facts. There are many kinds of petrels, I am reminded by my ornithologist critic. In deference to him I have changed "stormy" several times so as to conform to the facts—Kaeding's for instance, is the petrel on Three Arch Rocks in the Pacific, the stormy ("storm" alas! By the latest A.O.U. Check-List) petrel being an Atlantic bird nesting on the European side and only a rare wanderer to our shores. "Kaeding's" is the petrel of this chapter; according to the book; it may be, but not according to the poem, and when I read this chapter I shall read "stormy," whatever the unimaginative type says.

Leach's Petrel, Bohlman photograph, Three Arch Rocks

In an earlier chapter I have given a general description of Three Arch Rocks Reservation and its multitudes of wild sea-life, a description that falls hopelessly short of the scene. I had looked at pictures of the Rocks, had listened to stories of their rookeries, but the only account that had greatly interested me was of the small colony of petrels nesting on the steep north slope of the summit of Shag Rock, the outermost of the three. It was the petrels above all else that I desired to see; it was this patch of marl or earthy guano on the top of the rock that I wished to climb to; for this little patch of earth was something that I could share with the birds, a point upon which we could meet, a place that their wave wandering wings and my clod-heavy feet could have in common. The thought of it greatly moved me.

I must be something of a mariner. My forbears, back for three hundred years, have all been doctors, farmers, and the like; and Quakers of London before that. But the sea is in me, though I go back beyond the Vikings for it. And there is something of the stormy petrel in us all, I think, for who can meet the little mariner on the waves and not follow him up and down, up and down, till the wonderful wings bring him to Shag Rock?

Shag is an immense pile; not a pile of rocks, but single rude block of weathered basalt, longer than a city "block" and more than three hundred feet high. Wherever birds can find a foothold, and shelf enough for an egg, there they breed, a single pair, a rookery of thousands. The petrels nested on the top, coming and going only in the dark; and a night on the summit to see them come in to their burrows was to crown our trip to the Reservation.

Just to sleep in such a bed would be enough. To wrap one's self in one's blanket as the sun sinks behind the round of the Pacific, to see the night settle down upon the Rocks, to feel the large sea-wind sweep over the summit, to hear the swash of the ledges, the boom in the hollow caverns far below, and, close to one's head, the strange, wild clangor of the sea-birds—it would be enough to turn one's face to the mist in such a spot, and to know that one was part of this primordial life, cast up here, as the first life of the land had been cast, by the lift of the sea!

But how much more to lie here listening for the chitter of a small voice and for the fanning of small wings that know no dread, that have spanned the sweep of oceans, and outridden the wildest gales! I wanted to witness their coming home, to see, if possible, in the thick twilight of the summit, their shadows hovering over the slope, to hear their chittering at the mouth of the burrows, telling their mates that they had returned from their day and night upon the sea.

This petrel of Three Arch Rocks digs its nesting burrow in the earth and lays one egg. The burrow might hold both birds together, but only one bird is ever found in the nest-hole. While one is brooding, the other is off on its tireless wings—away off in the wake of your steamer, miles and miles from shore. All night it has been a-wing, and all day, but, as darkness begins to fall again, it remembers its mate and its nest on the rocks and speeds with the wing of the twilight to its own, to take its place in the little black burrow, while the mate comes forth and spreads her wings out over the darkening waters, not to return, it may be, until the day and the night have passed and dusk comes creeping once more over the sea.

But why waste words to make those who cannot understand know why we were willing to risk limb and life on the Rocks, not to mention the crossing of Tillamook Bar, in order to watch the coming and going of birds no larger than my hand? To them I speak in parables. And to you with hearts that understand I need not speak at all, for you know why we took the tug at Tillamook, why we fought for hours the three great breakers on the narrow, dangerous bar, why we steamed miles down the coast to the big rocks, where we landed amid the din of screaming gulls and bellowing sea-lions—why, in short, we never dreamed of counting the cost of watching for the petrels to come home on Shag Rock.

It is cheapest and safest, and, perhaps sanest, not to have any loves or enthusiasms. But it is also very stupid. A person so lacking might cross the ocean a hundred times and never see a stormy petrel. More than that, such a person might be too dull and mean and afraid ever to cross the ocean at all.

After steaming in around Shag Rock we landed from a yawl on a half-submerged ledge, driving off a bull sea-lion, an immense, disgruntled old fellow, who evidently could not live with the herd and his wretched temper, so had come out here where he could have his fill of soured silence and enjoy the solitary friendship of his precious ugly soul.

The rise and fall of the waves about the rocks was fully six feet, so we backed the yawl up as close as we dared, a man steadying it at the oars, another standing ready in the stern to leap when the sea should bring him up level with the ledge. Having landed him, we tossed him our cameras, provisions, a piece on every high wave, and even my eleven-year-old son, who scaled the rocks with us.

Everything safely cached, we drew the yawl upon the shelf of rock, ordered the tug to lie off and anchor, then got ourselves in shape for the climb.

It was now about noon. Since early morning an ugly fog had hung about us, but we had barely landed when the sun shot through the banks, promising us bright weather for our cameras, dry, safe footing on the cliffs, and a good night for watching on the peak.

It was hard to keep our heads on the way up with the birds driving at us, as it was hard to keep our feet on the rotten crumbling shelves and jutting corners that offered us their treacherous support. But my head was kept busy and out of mischief for most of the time with anxiety for my son, who showed no anxiety or ordinary human responsibility at all. We were mounting by ledge stages, each ledge the home of a colony of birds, and so thick with exciting eggs and young that the eleven-year-old boy was being forced to let go of one or was being held back from the other all the way. He climbed as if he had been hatched on the peak of Shag Rock. The rope about him was not necessary. Height and depth and the awful space about us held no terrors for him—such stuff is a live boy made of!

But all these things had terror enough for me, and I was glad to get over the rim, in reach of the top, although that gladness was troubled with the thought of how I was to get down. I had been brought up in the flat and gentle fields of New Jersey. I had climbed sand-dunes along the Jersey coast, and fences and trees, but never slippery, slimy bird rocks like these here in the Pacific.

Nothing I had ever seen on my native coast equaled this for wildness and strangeness and abundance of life. The very sea seemed vaster, no doubt because of the height of the rock, the mountains shoreward, and the bewildering, almost threatening, tumult of the alarmed birds spreading far out over the water.

While the cameras were being unslung and the moving picture machine set up, I went after the petrel's nests. It was now about three o'clock; the sun was hot and the young birds, especially the young cormorants, suffered from their exposure when our presence frightened their parents off the nests.

Never, from the time a cormorant egg is laid till the young fly from the nest, are the sheltering wings of the parents taken from them for fear of the greedy gulls. Our appearance had upset the even balance of things and was causing great disturbance and loss of life, though we moved without so much as breaking an egg.

Just below the rocky backbone of the top lay the green sloping deck or roof in which burrowed the puffins and the petrels. While digging out a snapping, fighting old puffin, who left the lasting mark of her powerful bill on the game warden's hand, I came upon a small side hall or gallery running at right angles to the gallery of the puffin's and starting just within her front door. At the bottom of this I found my first petrel and drew her out with her one round white egg, which was about the size of a turtle-dove's.

She lays only one egg, and rears only one young at a time. So it is with the puffin, and the murre; but just why, with food so abundant, I cannot tell. She tried to escape, but finding that impossible, she ejected from her beak, or nostrils rather, a very strong offensive oil, the most rancid oil I ever smelled. If her burrow were filled with this reeking, choking odor, I could imagine her perfectly safe from almost any attack.

I stoked her gently until she grew quiet. Then I stretched out her wonderful wings, placed her small webbed feet upon my hand, felt her beating heart between my thumb and finger, looked into her mild eyes, and tried to think that at last I held captive, in my hand, one of Mother Carey's chickens, "little Peter," the walker of the waves, the rider of curling crests, the lover of stormy seas.

But I could not think it. This was not the stormy petrel. This was only a small bunch of throbbing feathers—the least of all the web-footed birds. For so much greater is the power of the bird, so much mightier its spirit than its heartbeat and spread of wing, and with so much more had my imagination endowed her than with mere feathers and webbed feet, that I had to open my hand and free her in order to know that I had her—the bird of evil omen to the sailor, harbinger of foul weather, spirit of the sea wind and the wave.

She darted from my hand with a quick zigzag motion, as if dazzled with the sunshine, dipped over the rim of the top and with a flap was gone.

There was not a ray of sunshine, as a matter of fact, when I turned from following the bird to look at the sky. The afternoon was still young, yet the sun had disappeared, and the air, so thick with wings, was thickening now with fog that again was rolling in from seaward, blotting out the skyline and shutting darkly down about the gray, wild rocks.

The men packed their cameras, and, slipping into their coats, crept to shelter behind the peak, for a wind had come up with the fog, a raw, raking wind that drove the gulls careening far to leeward of the summit and forced them close to the sea for a landing.

The captain had warned us that a storm from this quarter might continue for a week, and it did look as if the whole Pacific were bearing down on us. The fog soon changed to a drizzle, and this in turn to a driving slant, that forced me to crawl from point to point about the peak.

It was not a pleasant prospect for the night. Besides, it would be quite impossible either to see or to hear the petrel's return in the pitch dark that was falling, and in the wind that was already drowning the lesser sounds—the screaming birds overhead, the wash of the waves, and the hollow boom of the caverns from below. No one could tell with what violence it might sweep this unsheltered top of Shag Rock, to the peril even of our lives.

There was nothing to do but climb down. It would surely clear by tomorrow, and, consoling ourselves, and particularly the eleven-year-old boy, with this hope, we backed over the edge of the peak for the descent.

The rocks were wet by this time, and the footing treacherous. The birds, as we worked slowly along, seemed to fear us less than earlier in the day, flying closer to our heads, their harsh cries and flapping wings in the gathering dusk adding not a little to the strain of the work.

Yet worse than the birds over me, was the emptiness behind me, the void and space beneath, which plucked and pulled at me, and which I could not turn upon and face. I could only reach down into it with a foot, feel out through it for an edge, a point, a seam of firm rock, anything to touch and stay me on.

Over the hanging places I was lowered with a rope, and down to me, bumping serenely along, his free hand patting all the little murres by the way, came Eleven Years. He wished to stay on the summit because it was storming; and wouldn't they tie him so fast that while dangling from the face of the cliffs he could use both hands freely to handle and examine eggs and young birds?

About forty feet from the water was a weathered niche partly roofed with rock, and with a floor large enough to give us a sleeping place. Here we stopped to wait for morning.

This was not the wild summit, nor were the rookeries of murres and the gulls whistling and quacking near us the stormy petrels we had hoped to see, but it was the wildest spot that I had ever tried to go to sleep in. For a time the lantern of the tug showed off on the sea, but this, too, was soon snuffed out by the fog, and we were alone in the midst of the waters with only the sea-lions and the sea-fowl and the pounding waves in the arches to lull us into slumber. But I could not sleep. I was afraid I might miss something of it all. For wings were heard passing in the darkness, and now and then a form was seen hurtling past. Might they not be petrels, I wondered. But they passed too swiftly through the shadows to be made out. I would wait for tomorrow.

I am still waiting.

The next day brought more wet and wind and chill. There might be a week of it, our prophet had said; and there was a week of it, as it turned out. The captain steamed in that afternoon and took us off, amid the din of a million screaming, bellowing voices.

The next time I climb Shag Rock I shall go storm-proof; for I yet intend to hear the winnowing wings of Mother Carey's chickens as they come in from the sea to take their turn on the nest.

Chapter
IV   The Wild Mother

Sharp's "Wild Mother," an article about a female murre he encountered on Shag Rock, first appeared in *Atlantic Monthly* in 1913. This account is made even more vivid because William Finley photographed Sharp with the bird.

I hear the bawling of my neighbor's cow. Her calf was carried off yesterday, and since then, during the long night, and all day long, her insistent woe had made our hillside melancholy. But I shall not hear her tonight, not from this distance. She will lie down tonight with the others of the herd, and munch her cud. Yet, when the rattling stanchions grow quiet and sleep steals along the stalls, she will turn her ears at every small stirring; she will raise her head to listen and utter a low tender moo. Her full udder hurts; but her cud is sweet. She is only a cow.

Had she been a wild cow, or had she been out with her calf in a wild pasture, the mother in her would had lived for six months. Here in the stable it will be forced to forget in a few hours, and by morning will have died.

There is a mother principle alive in all nature which never dies. This is different from the mother instinct, the mother principle. It is a law of life; it is one of the constants of being. The mother instinct or passion, on the other hand, occurs only among the higher animals; occurs not sporadically quite, for it is common enough; yet while generally found, and while one of the strongest, most interesting, most beautiful of animal traits, it is at the same time the most individual and the least constant.

On one of the large estates here in Hingham, a few weeks ago, a fox was found to be destroying poultry. The time of the raids, and their boldness, were proof enough that the fox must be a female with young. Poisoned meat was prepared for her, and at once the raids ceased. A few days later one of the workmen of the estate came upon the den of a fox, at the mouth of which lay dead a whole litter of young ones. They had been poisoned. The mother had not eaten the doctored food herself, but had carried it home to her family. They must have died in the burrow, for it was evident from the signs that she had dragged them out into the fresh air, to revive them, and deposited them gently on the sand by the hole. Then in her perplexity she had brought various tidbits of mouse and bird and rabbit and placed at their noses to tempt them to wake up out of their strange sleep and eat as hungry children ought to eat. Who knows how long she watched beside the still forms, and what her emotions were? She must have left the neighborhood soon after, however, for no one has seen her since about the estate.

I have elsewhere told of the cat, Calico, and her strange family; the thwarted cat mother making good the loss of her kittens by adopting a nest of young gray squirrels. A similar story comes to me from a reader in New York State. I will quote my correspondent's letter verbatim, not because there is an item in her account, remarkable as it is, that the most careful and experienced of observers would find hard to credit, but because it reads so much like a page out of the "Natural History of Selborne."

She writes:

"Our Tootsy became a mother of several little kittens; as she was not in the best of health we thought best not to let her raise any of them. For a day or two she mourned for her little ones. As she was the pet of the family, we consoled her as best we could. This day I had her out on the lawn. I looked down to the bridge, saw a little squirrel up on one of the bridge posts. I picked Tootsy up and let her climb the post to catch the squirrel, thinking it would take her mind off from her grief for a while.

"She brought it up on the lawn, and in place of playing with it and finally eating it, as is the nature of cats, she wanted to mother it. We then left her, and soon we discovered she had taken it upstairs in mother's bed and hid it. She stayed with it all night, and we saw the little squirrel could take nourishment.

"The next day she found two more squirrels and brought them

home, so we had a family of three. She brought them up until they were able to eat, meanwhile giving loads of pleasure; when they became so large and frisky we could do nothing with them, they would get into everything. We kept one, which disappeared shortly after. We think it had gotten with other squirrels, for sometimes when it did get out on the trees the cat would sit under the tree for hours at a time coaxing it back."

I have known a hen, too, deprived of her chicks, to adopt a litter of tiny kittens, brooding them and guarding them as her own.

The birds are structurally lower than the most primitive of the mammals; they are close kin to the cold hearted reptiles, yet it is the bird, the mother bird, rather, that has touched our imaginations as perhaps the most nearly human of all wild things.

The bird mother is the bravest, tenderest, most solicitous, most appealing thing one ever comes upon in the fields; the problem of her presence or absence, the degree or intensity of her being, and her behavior under stress, add more than anything else to the interest and charm of bird study. It is the rare exception, but we sometimes find the mother instinct wholly lacking among the birds, as in the case of our notorious cowbird, who sneaks about, watching her chance when some smaller bird is gone, to drop her egg into its nest. The egg must be laid; the burden of the race has been put upon the cowbird, but not the precious burden of the child. Hers are only the functions of maternity. She is not a mother. She is body only, not a soul.

The same is true of the European cuckoo, but not quite true of our American cuckoos, in spite of popular belief. For our birds (both species) build rude, elementary nests as a rule, and brood their eggs. Occasionally they may steal a robin's or a catbird's nest, may even destroy the owner's eggs (though never to my knowledge), in order to save labor—the unimaginative labor of laying one stick across another when one does not know how. But here is a plain case of knowledge waiting on desire. So undeveloped is the mother in the cuckoo that if you touch her eggs she will leave them—abandon her crude nest and eggs, as if any excuse were excuse enough for an escape from the cares of motherhood. How should a bird with so little mother love ever learn to build a firm-walled, safe, and love-lined nest?

The great California condor, according to the records of the only one ever studied, is a most faithful and anxious mother, the dumb affection of both parents indeed, for their single offspring, being at times pathetically human. On the other hand, the mother in the turkey buzzard is so evenly balanced against the vulture in her that I have known a brooding bird to be entirely undone by the sudden approach of a man and to rise from off her eggs and devour them instantly, greedily, and then make off on her serenely soaring wings into the clouds.

Such bird mothers, however, are not the rule. The buzzard, the cuckoo, and the cowbird are striking exceptions. The flicker will keep on laying eggs as fast as you take them from the nest hole, until she has no more eggs to lay. The quail, like the cuckoo, will sometimes desert her nest if even an egg is so much as touched, but only because she knows that her nest has been discovered and must be started anew, in some more hidden place, for safety. She is a wise and devoted mother, keeping her brood with her as a "covey" all winter long.

Gilbert White tells the following story of the raven's mother love:

"In the center of this grove there stood an oak, which, though shapely and tall on the whole, bulged out into a large excrescence about the middle of the stem. On this a pair of ravens had fixed their residence for such a series of years that the oak was distinguished by the title of the Raven Tree. Many were the attempts of the neighboring youths to get at this eyrie: the difficulty whetted their inclinations, and each was ambitious of surmounting the arduous task. But when they arrived at the swelling, it jutted out so in their way, and was so far beyond their grasp, that the most daring lads were awed, and acknowledged the undertaking to be too hazardous: so the ravens built on, nest upon nest, in perfect security, till the fatal day arrived in which the wood was to be leveled. It was in the month of February, when the birds usually sit. The saw was applied to the butt, the wedges were inserted into the opening, the woods echoed to the heavy blow of the beetle or mall or mallet, the tree nodded to its fall; but still the dam sat on. At last, when it gave way, the bird was flung from her nest, and, though her parental affection deserved a better fate, was whipped down by the twigs, which brought her dead to the ground."

One of the most interesting instances of variation of the mother instinct in the same species of birds, which has ever come under my observation, occurred in the rookeries of the Three Arch Rocks Reservation off the coast of Oregon.

We had gone out to the Reservation, as I said in the opening chapter, in order to study and photograph its wild life, and were making our slow way toward the top of the outer rock. Up the sheer south face of the cliff we had climbed, through rookery after rookery of nesting birds, until we reached the edge of the blade like back, or top, that ran up to the peak. Scrambling over this edge, we found ourselves in the midst of a great colony of nesting murres—hundreds of them—covering the steep, rocky part of the top.

As our heads appeared above the rim, many of the colony took wing and whirred over us out to sea, but most of them sat close, each bird upon her egg or over her chick, loath to leave, and so expose to us her hidden treasure.

The top of the rock was somewhat cone shaped, and in order to reach the peak, and the colonies on the west side, we had to make our way through this rookery of the murres. The first step among them, and the whole colony was gone, with a rush of wings and feet that sent several of the top-shaped eggs rolling, and several of the young birds toppling, over the cliff to the pounding waves and the ledges far below.

We stopped instantly. We had not come to frighten and kill. Our climb up had been very disturbing to the birds, and had been attended with some loss of both eggs and young. This we could not help; and we had been too much concerned for our own lives really to notice what was happening. But here on the top, with the climb beneath us, the sight of a young murre going over the rim, clawing and clinging with beak and nails and unfledged wings, down from jutting point to shelf, to ledge, down, down—the sight of it made one dizzy and sick.

We stopped, but the colony had bolted, leaving scores of eggs and scores of downy young squealing and running together for shelter, like so many beetles under a lifted board.

But the birds had not every one bolted, for here sat two of the colony among the broken rocks. These two had not been frightened off. That both of them were greatly alarmed, any one could see from

Sharp approaching female murre

their open beaks, their rolling eyes, their tense bodies on tiptoe for flight. Yet here they sat, their wings out like props, or more like gripping hands, as if they were trying to hold themselves down to the rocks against their wild desire to fly.

And so they were in truth, for under their extended wings I saw little black feet moving. Those two mother murres were not going to forsake their babies—no, not even for fear of these approaching monsters, which had never been seen clambering over their rocks before!

One of the monsters stood stock still a moment for the other one, the photographer, to come up. Then both of them took a step nearer. It was very interesting. I had often come slowly up to quail on their nests, and to other birds. Once I crept upon a killdeer in a bare field until my fingers were almost touching her. She did not move because she thought I did not see her, it being her trick thus to hide within her own feathers, colored as they are to blend with the pebbly fields where she lays her eggs. So the brown quail also blends with its brown grass nest. But those murres, though colored in harmony with the rocks, were still, not because they hoped I did not see them. I did see them. They knew it. Every bird in the great colony had known it, and had gone—with the exception of these two.

What was different about these two? They had their young ones to protect. But so had every bird in the great colony its young one, or its egg, to protect; yet all the others had gone. Did these two have more love than the others, and with it, or because of it, more courage, more intelligence?

We took another step toward them, and one of the two birds sprang into the air, knocking her baby over and over with the stroke of her wing, coming within an inch of hurling it across the rim to be battered on the ledges below. The other bird raised her wings to follow, then clapped them back over her baby. Fear is the most contagious thing in the world; and that flap of fear by the other bird thrilled her too, but as she withstood the stampede of the colony, so she caught herself again and held on.

She was now alone on the bare top of the rock, with ten thousand circling birds screaming to her in the air above, and with two men creeping up to her with a big black camera which clicked ominously. She let the multitude scream, and with threatening beak watched the two men come on. A motherless baby, spying her, ran down the rock squealing for his life. She spread her wing, put her bill behind him, and shoved him quickly in out of sight with her own baby. The man with the camera saw the act, for I heard his machine click, and I heard him say something under his breath that you would hardly expect a mere man and a game warden to say. But most men have a good deal of the mother in them; and the old bird had acted with such decision, such courage, such swift, compelling instinct, that any man, short of the wildest savage, would have felt his heart quicken at the sight.

Just how compelling might that mother instinct be? I wondered. Just how much would that mother love stand?

I had dropped to my knees, and on all fours had crept up within about three feet of the bird. She still had a chance for flight. Would she allow us to crawl any nearer? Slowly, very slowly, I stretched forward on my hands, like a measuring worm, until my body lay flat on

Sharp with female murre

the rocks, and my fingers were within three inches of her. But her wings were twitching; a wild light danced in her eyes; and her head turned itself toward the sea.

For a whole minute I did not stir. Then the wings again began to tighten about the babies; the wild light in the eyes died down; the long, sharp beak turned once more toward me. Then slowly, very slowly, I raised by hand, and gently touched her feathers with the tip of one finger—with two fingers—with my whole hand, while the loud camera click-clacked, click-clacked hardly four feet away!

It was a thrilling moment. I was not killing anything. I had no high powered rifle in my hands, coming up against the wind toward an unsuspecting creature hundreds of yards away. This was no wounded leopard charging me; no mother bear defending with her giant might a captured cub. It was only a mother bird, the size of a wild duck, with swift wings at her command, hiding under those wings her own and another's young, and her own boundless fear!

For the second time in my life I had taken captive with my bare hands a free wild bird. No, I had not taken her captive. She had made herself a captive; she had taken herself in the strong net of her mother love.

And now her terror seemed quite gone. At the first touch of my hand she felt, I think, the love restraining it, and without fear or fret allowed me to push my hand under her and pull out the two downy babies. But she reached after them with her bill to tuck them back out of sight, and when I did not let them go, she sidled toward me, quacking softly—a language that I perfectly understood, and was quick to answer.

I gave them back, fuzzy, and black and white. She got them under her, stood up over them, pushed her wings down hard around them, her stout tail down hard behind them, and together with them pushed in an abandoned egg which was close at hand. Her own baby, some one else's baby, and someone else's forsaken egg! She could cover no more; she had not feathers enough. But she had heart enough; and into her mother's heart she had already tucked every motherless egg and nestling of the thousands of frightened birds that were screaming and wheeling in the air high over her head.

Chapter
V   The Raven
Of The Deshutes

In early July the Finley/Sharp party left Portland by train for eastern Oregon. Their jump off point into the desert would be Bend, in what is known as Central Oregon. The rail line follows the Deschutes River upward to Bend. In a letter to his wife back at Jennings Lodge, Sharp recounted his progress, and mentioned seeing a raven which formed the idea for a book chapter. He was writing this chapter during a period when some of the most important actions were being carried out for the preservation of wildlife, such as the very significant Weeks-McLean bill of 1913. Sharp was optimistic in this chapter. Unfortunately, the heath hens of which he wrote on Martha's Vineyard became extinct in 1932-1933.

Dear Grace and dear Boys—

If just 5 more persons than me at Jennings Lodge were right here with me listening to the rush of the Deschutes River through its mighty canyon then I could ask nothing. But it takes just those 5 to make the river sound right, and the canyon to look right, and the whole wonderful day's journey to be all right—no slang intended!

We are stopping a few minutes at Hunts Ferry, 167 miles from Portland, & 61 miles up from Deschutes Crossing where we left the main line of the Northern Pacific—the very route over which we will start home.

The Deschutes is a clear rapid stream running down hard all the way with many small falls to the Columbia—having cut its way down into a canyon for a thousand feet—with rim rock edges half a mile wide. The walls are hazy purple where they are all rock & velvety greenish gold sugar loaf shape and cut with many small canyons where the soil is covered with grass. No trees except a single line in places right at the water's edge—no houses, no sign of habitation—only the continuous curving railroad & the great towering rocks or the sloping walls of buttes—just like the pictures of the Bad Lands or the Colorado River Canyon. Sage brush, gray & dusty grows thin on the sides & in the narrow stony bottom, but there is no mead-

49

ow, no growing crops—the two rural RR lines having worked their way along the face of the canyon to Bend all for the sake of the country beyond.

Here & there a cattle trail or a wagon road creeps down on the long slant along the face of the canyon from the unseen world of table land—wild grazing country—above, the trail or road looking like a gutter or rain pipe aslant some great house from the corner of the roof to the diagonal corner at the ground. The rocks are often beautifully columnar—basalt I suppose— like those pictured in the geography off the coast of Ireland or Scotland—"The Giant's Causeway"? Way up on one inaccessible cliff stood a raven, black, lonely, suggestive, watching us pass. His nest was near at hand no doubt for here is where they breed.

We won't get to Bend until 9 tonight—where we will stay till a.m., then start on the auto stage for Burns. Doves, western kingbirds, fish hawks & sparrow hawks have been seen in the canyon & back where the rocks rise sheer & high from the water a great flock of nesting cliff swallows

(page 4 of letter missing)

(start page 5) *by way of Trout Creek, a branch of the Deschutes, and are in the rolling sage brush country still in a broad valley with here & there a bunch of cattle, a lone farm & golden wheat field with the harvester at work, while the jackrabbits are jumping over themselves & then as we climb higher over the tablelands to the edge of the world treeless, houseless rolls the vast vastland.*

6:30 we are up still higher (passing "Paxton"—one house & station) and the great sections of the sage brush are giving way to wheat & corn & real farm buildings—one! For the rest—the few shacks are not fit for humans, & life at such cost seems hardly so good at Salem St. and the slums. But it is wide & large & silent & long with future up here & might easily breed great men.

Mt. Jefferson is straight ahead—with the 3 Sisters (of the Cascade range off to the left) with the town of Madras near at hand. Here at Madras is the auto—and yet the jackrabbits eat off large corners & big holes in the wheatfields!

Metolius—40 miles from Bend—150 miles from Bend to Burns to be taken by auto tomorrow. We have just had supper here at Metolius & I will stop this double-track tale of the trip to post it at Bend with a prayer for

*your safe keeping at Jennings Lodge & for the good Lord to deliver me from
this noble land of treeless wheat fields just as the sun goes down! I like
Hingham better. With lots & lots of love & wishes that you were with me.
Dallas & Father*

*PS: Keep this letter as it is letter & notes in one. All the account of the day I
have. Love—lots more. D.S.*

*PS:2 Tramp around the cucumber vines & hoe them. Hoe the tomato vines
back of barn—please.*

THE RAVEN OF THE DESCHUTES

As our train clung to its narrow footing and crept slowly up
the wild canon of the Deschutes, I followed from the rear plat
form the windings of the milk-white river through its carved
course. We had climbed along some sixty miles to where the folding
walls were sheerest and the towering treeless buttes rolled, fold upon
fold, behind us on the sky, when, off from one of the rim rock ledges,
far above, flapped a mere blot of a bird, black, and strong of wing,
flying out into midair between the cliffs to watch us, and sailing back
upon the ledge as we crawled round a jutting point in the wall and
passed from his bight of the deep wild gorge.

Except for some small birds in the willows of the river, this was
the first glimpse of life that I had seen since entering the canyon.
And I knew, though this was my first far off sight of the bird, that I
was watching a raven. Beside him on the ledge was a gray blur that I
made out to be a nest—an ancient nest, I should say, from the stains
below it on the face of the rock.

A fleck of black high up against the cliff, he yet seemed to fill the
canyon. The shadow of his wings, as he flew out in the sky to watch
us pass, spread up and down the valley. The smoke of our engine
would quickly disappear, but the shadow of the raven's authority was
the very air of these cliffs and bluffs and buttes, the spell that we had
felt since the mighty walls had first shut in about us.

Or did I imagine it all? This is a treeless country, green with
grass, yet, as for animal life, an almost uninhabited country. When

Lewis and Clark passed here, they could find not sticks for camp fires and lived on dog meat—so utterly without life were the hills and headlands of the river. Such lack of wild life had seemed incredible; but no longer so after entering the canon of the Deschutes. A deep, unnatural silence filled the vast spaces between the beetling walls and smothered the roar of the rumbling train. The river, one of the best trout streams in the world, broke white and loud over a hundred stony shallows, but what wild creature, besides the osprey, was here to listen? The softly rounded buttes, towering above the river, and running back beyond the cliffs, were greenish gold against the sky, with what seemed clipped grass, like to some golf links of the gods; but no creature of any kind moved over them. Bend after bend, mile after mile, and still no life, except a few small birds in the narrow willow edging where the river made about some sandy cove. That was all—until out from his eyrie in the overhanging rim rock flapped the raven.

The canyon was no longer empty, the towering buttes no longer bare. This was the domain of the black baron, and he held it all. No lesser land, no tamer, gentler country would fit him, somber, suspicious, unsociable, uncanny croaker of the strong black wing! It was here that I had hoped to find him, knowing that to such remote and rugged regions he had withdrawn to make his nest and live his life. How his silent flight, his black body on the shelf of the rock high up in the canyon wall, have shape and substance to the spirit of the place! If the fir trees are a house for the stork, and the high hills a refuge for the wild goats, no less is the steep walled canon and the dizzy mountain cliff the home of the raven.

Yet the raven is the head of the tribe of crows, with all the intelligence and cunning of the crow, but lacking, it seems, the crow's easy disposition and sociable ways. Else why is it that he does not adapt himself, as the crow does, to human ways? Are we at fault? Not wholly, for we could hardly treat him worse than we have the crow. Perhaps the crows are becoming fewer; I think they are. The wonder is that a single crow is still alive in the land after all their years of persecution. But here they are, cawing in my wood lot this quiet November day, as I have heard them since I can remember hearing anything. Here in my pines they nest too. Could not the raven nest here, and croak here, with them?

So far as I am concerned he could. Nay, I would give him a whole wood lot for a nest if he would come. For should I not find him, as I have at last found the crow, to be my friend and ally, instead of my enemy?

A new and better day has dawned for the birds, all birds. The greatest event, surely, that has ever happened for American birds took place on the 4th day of March, 1913, when President Taft signed the Weeks-McLean bill placing all our migratory game and insectivorous birds under the protection of the Federal Government; and perhaps the greatest event that ever happened for the birds of the world took place on the night of September 3, 1913, when the United States Senate passed a measure prohibiting the importation of the plumage of wild birds into this country, except for scientific purposes.

Neither of these bills will directly protect the crow, except as they are sure to help protect all birds. But the crow will be cared for. The Government's book on the crow shows past all doubt that he is, in the long run, beneficial; that we are tremendously in his debt, notwithstanding his toll of corn; and that he must not only be allowed to dwell among us, but encouraged by every means to make himself free with our fields and wood lots.

And he will do it without encouragement. All he asks is decent neighborly treatment. He will meet us more than halfway. The light and the laws have come too late for many of our birds—for those that have gone forever from the earth. The State of Massachusetts has a game warden on the Island of Martha's Vineyard, who, as I am writing, is policing the haunts of the few wild heath hens there, the last survivors of a noble family of grouse that, hardly a hundred years ago, was found locally throughout southern New England and the Middle States. Have the laws and the light come too late for the heath hen?

Perhaps with this remnant we can yet save the race. In 1890 it was estimated that there were from 120 to 200 birds on the island. A few years later (1907), they had been so nearly exterminated, that only 21 were found to have escaped. Today (1913) some three or four hundred are reported from the island. If the light and laws have not come too late, the heath hen, from this mere handful, may be increased until they have scattered themselves once more over their former haunts.

But what can we ever do for the raven? And for the birds of prey? And for such solitary creatures as the great California condor, now on the verge of extinction?

As for the great condor, he is passing from the peaks of his mountain home because he is being wantonly shot. His great spread of wings is a mark for the hunter. He is being shot for the mark's sake, his carcass left to rot where it falls; while from the skies of the Sierra are snatched forever the most thrilling wings that shall ever coast the clouds.

It seems certain that the eagles and the greater hawks must pass, as being unfit for a civilized scheme of things. But the owls and the lesser hawks should remain, and along with them the wilder, shyer, more suspicious birds like the raven.

Shall he need to be educated? Or is nothing more necessary than that we show him our good faith? It may be that I have misunderstood his mind toward me. Perhaps I read things into his character that I found in a book—

"Once upon a midnight dreary,"

—when I was a child. Perhaps I have Poe's raven and the raven of the Deschutes canon mixed in my mind. But I watched him in the desert rim rock country, and there he seemed to be the most aloof, the most alien in his attitude, of all wild things I have ever seen. In the high rim rock ledges of the Blitzen River valley I watched several flocks of the big, black birds. Two specimens were shot for their skins, and for what we could learn of their feeding habits from the contents of their gizzards. One of the birds fell at my feet, his strong, wild spirit gone, and only the black form left, with its powerful beak and wise, crafty face. But even this body I took up and touched with a feeling of wonder and something akin to awe.

Surely he is too wise a bird to be driven from his inheritance because of fear of us. The grizzly bears come and go at will in the Yellowstone National Park because they know we mean no harm. The fierce spirit of the beast is led about by gentleness and by good faith, kept inviolate. If the bear, why not the raven?

John Muir, speaking of the Clarke crow of the high Sierra, a relation of the raven, says: "He dwells far back on the high storm beaten margin of the forest, where the mountain pine, juniper, and hemlock grow wide apart on glacier pavements and domes and rough crumbling ridges, and the dwarf pine makes a low crinkled growth along the flanks of the Summit peaks. In so open a region, of course, he is well seen. Everybody notices him, and nobody at first knows what to make of him. One guesses he must be a woodpecker; another crow or some sort of jay; another magpie. He seems to be a pretty thoroughly mixed and fermented compound of all these birds, has all their strength, cunning, shyness, thievishness, and wary, suspicious curiosity combined and condensed."

I took it from this account that if in my mountain climbing I got a long distance glimpse of the Clarke crow, I could count myself lucky, for isn't he the wildest of birds? On the contrary, I was amazed to find the wary creature almost eating out of my hand at Cloud Cap Inn, halfway up the side of Mount Hood. Here, on the timberline, in the haunts of these birds, was a house, and human visitors in the summer, who fed the crows, and who had so far tamed them as to make them almost as familiar as chickens, much more sociable and trusting than our Eastern blue jays or our common crows.

If this can be done to the Clarke crow in the remote summits, it ought to be possible to tame the raven till he will accept a ledge from our hands or a nest tree in our parks and groves, and with him tame every other shy, suspicious spirit that hides from hurt and destruction in the "holy mountain," when the knowledge and love of wild life shall cover the earth as the waters cover the sea.

English human life and wild life have arrived at a much closer sympathy and understanding than we, in this country, appreciate. Wildlife has been protected there for centuries, and there even the raven has held on in solitary pairs, occupying for generations the same ancient trees. It seems that gradually they are dying out and may pass forever. But the English people love their birds; and how often the raven comes in for his share, both of reproach and admiration, his historians without exception endowing him with a greatness of spirit that comes close to majesty!

There is no more interesting chapter in the lives of British birds than that on the raven. I have never read anything about our

American raven that shows the careful watching and the intimate knowledge of the following description of the English bird.

Says the writer:

"They will tag with one another in midair and often tumble down a fathom or two, as if shot, to turn right over on their backs, in sheer merriment; when the wind is high, the tempest loving birds shoot up in the air like a rocket or a towering partridge, to an immense height; and then, by closing their wings, drop, in a series of rapid jerks and plunges, which they can check at pleasure, down to the ground. The male raven, while his mate is sitting, keeps anxious watch over her, and croaks savagely when any one approaches, or sallies forth in eager tournament, against any rook, or crow, or hawk, or larger bird of prey which intrudes on his domain.

"If you can manage to evade his watchful eye, and enter the wood unobserved, you can, sometimes, lie down quite still, in sight of the nest and note all that is going on. You will see him perch upon the very top of an adjoining fir tree, or whet his beak, as he is fond of doing, against one of its branches, or fiercely tear off others and drop them below. You will hear him utter a low gurgling note of conjugal endearment, which will, sometimes, lure his mate from her charge, and then, after a little coze and talk together, you will see him, unlike many husbands, relieve her, for the time, of her responsibilities, and take his own turn upon the nest."

The raven has but one mate; he pairs for life, and as he lives to a very great age, the strength of his affection, his tenderness and fidelity impart to him a dignity and a quality of character hardly possessed by any other bird.

All this seems to be based on a superior degree of intelligence, a quality of mind that shows itself among all the members of the raven family. It is especially noticeable among the crows. There are no other birds in my woods that seem half so intelligent and wise as they. Watch the ways of your tame crow, study the light in his eye, especially when he is up to mischief, if you would see a mind within that is pretty nearly human.

Or watch the blue jays or the magpies or the whiskey jacks— "camp robbers," as they are called. These lovely fluffy birds of the Canadian woods and wild Western mountains are, I think, the smallest of the family. I had an excellent chance to study their doings in the Wallowa Mountains. No other bird of equal curiosity and intelligence have I ever seen. Far off in the most distant wilderness, where possibly no human foot had trodden for months, we would camp, and immediately the robbers would gather, flapping out of some tall fir top across a meadow to light upon the tree top nearest to us. Here they would perch and squall, and find their way down to the sizzling frying pans, to see what sour dough bread was like, and if there might be anything left in the condensed milk tins.

Right out of the unbroken forest they came, straight down to the fire—because they wanted to know what they didn't understand. The interest (curiosity, if you choose), the confidence, the impertinence, indeed, seemed so unnatural, unbirdlike, here where all was wild, as to be almost uncanny. No crow or raven would go to that length, because the years of persecution have taught them to temper their curiosity with extreme caution; but both birds, and all members of the family, are at heart friendly, and would get on well with us, would we show ourselves neighborly.

And they shall get on with us. For the first time since the slaughter of wild life began on these shores the country as a whole has been aroused to the need of instant and country-wide protection. The Federal Government has acted. As I am writing these lines, the custom house officers are snipping off the lovely aigrettes from the hats brought into our ports from abroad. The women are weeping and wringing their hands and doing more violent things at the wicked destruction of the costly plumes; but could they see the white heron rookeries with the heaps of rotting carcasses, and the nests of piping, starving young, could they see the plumes stripped from the brooding mothers' backs, they would understand; and no more would they make themselves the occasion for such cruel, unspeakable destruction.

And so it will soon be with us in our feeling for the new federal laws prohibiting the shooting of the migratory birds. A few hunters think that their rights (to kill the wild birds that fly over and belong to us all, but to no one person) are being encroached upon. But they will learn better soon. And soon we shall all of us learn better how to live with the birds and other wild things, and let them live with us.

We are only beginning to realize our deep dependence upon our wild neighbors, and the birds especially. As this knowledge grows, and as our love for wild life grows, we shall draw closer and closer together, we shall share and share alike, birds and beasts and men, all the things we have. We shall even learn to make all of our aigrettes— of horsehair! Then in that day (if he can find him a dwelling place until that day comes) even the raven, the wild black prince of birds, shall build his nest without fear of the trains that thunder through the canon far below him, and without harm from the shepherds whose flocks feed in the sage back on the wide plains above.

Chapter
VI   From Bend to Burns

Today, even with the paved highway, the trip from Bend to Burns is a long one. In 1912 it must have been remarkable. Sharp wrote his wife once he arrived in Burns. Of interest, he used stationery from the Hotel Bend, Hugh O'Kane, Manager. The letterhead stated: "Headquarters for commercial men. Free bus to and from all trains." The stationery also contained the following about Bend in 1912, now one of Oregon's favorite cities:

Bend is situated in the very heart of the Deschutes Valley, on the banks of the Deschutes River where the vast pine timber belt meets the irrigated lands. No other town in all Central Oregon is so well located for economic development, no other can approach it in the beauty and health-fulness of its surroundings, and none will be half so much benefitted by the coming of the railroads.

A great irrigation segregation has its headquarters at Bend. At least twenty billion feet of timber is tributary to the town, whose milling in itself assures a great future. The Deschutes river in the immediate vicinity offers some 25,000 horsepower for the operation of the mills and plants of the future.

Bend is the present terminus of the Oregon Trunk Railroad and of the Harriman Deschutes Railroad. The east and west line of the Hill road branches off from the Columbia-Klamath line at Bend. Bend, then, is situated at what will be the most important junction point in Oregon.

Immediately adjacent to Bend are some three hundred thousand acres of irrigated land under the Carey Act segregation of the Central Oregon Irrigation Company. The land is FREE. Perpetual water rights cost $40 an acre. Forty acres means independence, eighty acres brings wealth. Every product adapted to the temperate zone thrives in the rich volcanic soil. The land is easily worked and watered. It offers the greatest irrigationist's oppor-tunity to be found in the Northwest. Come and investigate for yourself before all the big cheap land chances are gone.

From Bend settlers are located on 320 acre homesteads on the vast area of sage brush lands to the southwest. Here is found the biggest and the last big chance for the land hungry to get free Government land that is worth having.

The railroads are here. Hurry and get in on the ground floor. Central Oregon is the greatest homeseeker's and investor's proposition in all the West today. Bend is the pivot point of Central Oregon. It is destined to make a magnificent city. Those who come to Bend now and to the country around Bend, will win wonderful rewards for their foresight.

And when you come to Bend remember that the HOTEL BEND IS THE PLACE TO STOP."

Once in Burns, Sharp wrote:

We expect to go from here to Harney & Malheur lakes to see grebes & white herons, then out to Silver Lake, then back to P Ranch, then down into Steins Mts. for Mt. sheep. Then on west to Warner Lake for antelope, then up to Summer Lake & on across the desert back to Bend—fully a week yet. I am sorry to be away so long, sorry you can't all have this trip, only it is impossibly expensive, & impossibly long & remote for any but those who can get such matters as I am after. I think I got 3 good stories yesterday. Two of them sketches & one real story. The trip over must make an Atlantic article. The story will be good for Youth Companion *sketch.*

The story happened toward mid afternoon 55 miles away in the desert when a rancher came galloping across the sage brush & halted us saying "I've got a man back here who is dying, can you take him in?" We were loaded, the fellow was dying with appendicitis for needed operation. No one wanted to drop out and stay, no one knows how long to give the poor devil his place. No one wanted him to die! Do you see the story? A daisy. But the real story was funny. As we stood in the presence of death and our duty up behind us came the 2nd stage (they started us in pairs) and in it was a doctor! He put in quick to the ranch & came out with a grin all over his face. "What is it Doctor" I asked. "Oh, its on the wrong side for appendicitis." It turned out to be a severe strain from roping horses from a wild herd! But I've a picture & a sensation for a real story for I lived one there in that desolate waste the few minutes we were sizing up the situation. So I don't believe it can turn out a failure—the trip I mean—for me. I am seeing a new setting for lots of future things.

I am sending you a picture of snow geese. Put the microscope on them, there are a million nearly in this single flock, this is the way they still swarm in winter over Harney Valley.

I may not get to write again for days as we are on the road away off from RR. But send me letter here. I may be back. Do take care. Keep well— but let me hope that I can make all this enlarge all our outlook later on by my pen.

Kisses & love to all. Dallas.

FROM BEND TO BURNS

The clutch snapped in with a jump; forward, backward shot the lever—we were rounding a corner in a whirl of dust, Bend behind us, and the auto stage like some giant jack rabbit bounding through the sagebrush for Burns, one hundred and fifty miles across the desert.

Think of starting from New York for Wilmington, Delaware, or from Boston for New Haven, Connecticut, with nothing, absolutely nothing but sagebrush and greasewood and stony lava ridges and a barely discernible trail in between! With a homesteader's shack for Providence, another shack for Norwich, and sage, sage, sage!

It was the size of the West and the spirit of the West—this combination of sage and automobile—that struck me as most unlike things back East, size and spirit commensurate. The difference was not one of race or blood. The new Northwest has very largely come out of the older East, the same blood there as here; but a different spirit. Spirit is an elastic thing; and if we had the spaciousness of that western country, we should doubtless have the soul to fill it, as the little town of Burns fills it for a hundred and fifty miles of sage, whichever way you go.

We were "going in" from Bend, over the High Desert. We were to speak to the Rod and Gun Club of Burns. We were to visit the great Malheur Lake Reservation just south of Burns, and the vast wild lands of the Steins Mountains on farther south, which the State has since turned into a wild animal reservation. We were also bringing in with us a carload of young trout to stock the Silvies River and the creeks about Burns.

Bohlman on the way to Burns

Our telegram had gone around by Baker City, Sumpter, and Canon City; thence had been relayed by telephone to Burns; our carload of fingerling trout was to follow us by auto truck from Bend over the desert; and we—the July morning found us heading over an horizon of gray sage into the sunrise, the purplish pine stems of the Deschutes Forest Reservation far to south and west of us, and over them, in the far northwest, the snowy peaks of Jefferson and the Three Sisters.

There was nothing else to be seen; not at this point, that is, for we were but just starting, and were using all our eyes to hang on with.

I had never ridden from Bend to Burns by auto stage before, and I did not realize at first that you could hold yourself down by merely anchoring your feet under the rail and gripping everything in sight. It is a simple matter of using all your hands and knees and feet. But at the start I was wasting my strength, as, with eyes fixed and jaw set, I even held on to my breath in order to keep up with the car.

The desert was entirely new to me; so was the desert automobile. I had been looking forward eagerly to this first sight of the sage plains; but I had not expected the automobile, and could see nothing whatever of the sagebrush until I had learned to ride the car. I had ridden an automobile before; I had driven one, a staid and even going Eastern car, which I had left at home in the stable. I thought I knew an automobile; but I found that I had never been on one of the Western desert breed. The best bucker at the Pendleton Round Up is but a rocking horse in comparison. I doubt if you could experience death in any part of the world more times for twenty dollars than by auto stage from Bend to Burns.

The trail takes account of every possible bunch of sagebrush and greasewood to be met with on the way. It never goes over a bunch if it can go around a bunch; and as there is nothing but bunches all the way, the road is very devious. It turns, here and there, every four or five feet (perhaps the sagebrush clumps average five feet apart), and it has a habit, too, whenever it sees the homesteader's wire fences, of dashing for them, down one side of the claim, then short about the corner and down the other side of the claim, steering clear of all the clumps of sage, but ripping along horribly near to the sizzling barbs of the wire and the untrimmed stubs on the juniper posts; then darting off into the brush, this way, that way, every way, which in the end proves to be the way to Burns, but no one at the beginning of the trip could believe it—no one from the East, I mean.

The utter nowhereness of that desert trail! Of its very start and finish! I had been used to starting from Hingham and arriving—and I am two whole miles from the station at that. Here at Mullein Hill I can see South, East, and North Weymouth, plain Weymouth, and Weymouth Heights, with Queen Anne's Corner only a mile away; Hanover Four Corners, Assinippi, Egypt, Cohasset, and Nantasket are hardly five miles off; and Boston itself is but sixty minutes distant by automobile, Eastern time.

It is not so between Bend and Burns. Time and space are different concepts there. Here in Hingham you are never without the impression of somewhere. If you stop you are in Hingham; if you go on you are in Cohasset, perhaps. You are somewhere always. But between Bend and Burns you are always in the sagebrush and right on the distant edge of time and space, which seems by contrast with Hingham the very middle of nowhere. Massachusetts time and space, and doubtless European time and space, as Kant and Schopendauer maintained, are not world elements independent of myself, at all, but only a priory forms of perceiving. That will not do from Bend to Burns. They are independent things out there. You can whittle them and shovel them. They are sagebrush and sand, respectively. Nor do they function there as here in the East, determining, according to the metaphysicians, the sequence of conditions, and positions of objects toward each other; for the desert will not admit of it. The Vedanta well describes "the-thing-in-itself" between Bend and Burns in what it says of Brahman: that "it is not split by time and space and is free from all change."

That, however, does not describe the journey; there was plenty of change in that, at the rate we went, and according to the exceeding great number of sagebrushes we passed. It was all change; through all sage. We never really tarried by the side of any sagebrush. It was impossible to do that and keep the car shying rhythmically—now on its two right wheels, now on its two left wheels—past the sagebrush next ahead. Not the journey, I say; it is only the concept, the impression of the journey, that can be likened to Brahman. But that single, unmitigated impression of sage and sand, of nowhereness, was so entirely unlike all former impressions that I am glad I made the journey from Boston in order to go from Bend to Burns.

You lose no time getting at the impression. It begins in Bend—long before, indeed, being distributed generally all over this Oregon country. At Bend the railroad terminates. The only thing you can do at Bend is to go back—unless you are bound for Burns. The impression does not begin at Bend, and it does not end at Burns. It only deepens. For at Burns there is not so much as a railroad terminus. You cannot go back from Burns, or "out," as the citizens say, until there are enough of your mind to charter the auto stage. The next railroad terminus to Burns is Vale, east northeast one hundred and thirty-five miles of sage beyond.

Not split by time and space, and free from all change, single, deep, indelible, gray is the desert from Bend to Burns.

It was 7:10 in the morning when we started from Bend, it was after eight in the evening when we swung into Burns. At noon we halted for dinner at a rude road house, half the journey done; at one o'clock we started on with a half of it yet to go—at the same pace, over the same trail, through the same dust and sun and sage, the other car of our party, that had followed us so far, now taking the lead. There were details enough, there was variety enough, had one but the time and the eyes to see. I had neither. This was my first day in the desert; and it was the desert that I wanted to traverse—it was the sage and the sand, the roll, the reach of the horizon, the gray, sage gray, that I had come out to see. I must travel swift and look far off. For you cannot compass the desert horizon at a glance. Nor can you see at a glance this desert gray; it is so low a tone, a color so hard to fix. I must see sage gray until it should dye the very grain of my imagination, as the bitter flavor of the sage stains the blood, and tastes in the very flesh of sage hen.

A day was not long enough; one hundred and fifty speeding miles could not carry me fast enough or far enough to see the desert. And if I should stop to look for the desert life, for the parts, I should miss the whole. But I had my hand instinctively upon the driver's arm when a sage sparrow darted in front of the car. It was a new bird to me. Then a sage thrasher flitted away and alighted as the car sped past—another new bird! A badger drew into its burrow—I had never seen the badger at home; a lizard, a small horned toad, a gray and yellow winged grasshopper, a picket-pin—two—three of them—all new, all children of the desert! A little shrike, a cluster of squat golden balled flowers, a patch of purple things close to the sand giving a drop of color to the stretch of gray, a slender striped chipmunk, a small brown owl dangling between the sage clumps, and calling like a flicker, another at the mouth of an old badger's den——the burrowing owl, to be sure, and the first I have ever seen! *Whirr-r-r-r*—the great sage hen! And my hand shot out again—this time at the steering wheel. The driver only grunted, and opened the throttle a little wider if anything. He was not after sage hens; he was on the road to Burns.

If only he would blow out a tire! He did break a rear axle later on in the afternoon, and to my amazement and chagrin pulled a spare one out of his toolbox, and had it on as if it were part of the program. But he gave me a chance to start my first jack rabbit and send him careening over the plain. I crept up on a Western nighthawk, too: I gathered the most glorious of American primroses, white and as large as a morning glory, but an almost stemless flower like most of the desert plants. I snatched and threw into the car eight other new species of desert flowers; nibbled a leaf of sage and some of the salty shad scale; picked up a large fragment of black obsidian, and beside it a broken Indian arrowhead of the same lava glass; saw where a coyote had been digging out picket-pins; and was trying to capture a scorpion when the mended car overtook me—and on through the sage we rolled.

Another stop like this and my desert would be lost. One cannot watch a desert. But one can watch a scorpion; and to leave the only live scorpion I had ever seen was hard. As we whirled past a camping freighter, his horses outspanned in the sun, I envied him the ten days he was taking to cover what I was being hurled across in one. To freight it across the High Desert! To feel the beating sun at midday, and at midnight the bite of the frost! To waken in the unspeakable freshness of the cold dawn to the singing of the sage thrasher; and at twilight, the long desert twilight, to watch the life of the silent plains awaken, to hear the quaking call of the burrowing owls, and far off through the shadows the cry of the prowling coyotes!

If something else would happen to the car—something serious— all four axles at once! But it was not to be. We were destined to sleep in Burns—a restless sleep, however. I would much rather take my chances next time with the occasional scorpion in the sage. We were due in Burns that night. We were to speak to the Rod and Gun Club. We were to tell them that the carload of young fish would be on the road by midnight, that we had seen the truck at Bend; that they could expect the fish surely by evening of the next day.

On we sped into the sage, on into the lengthening afternoon; the scattered juniper trees, strangely like orchard trees at a distance, becoming more numerous, the level stretches more varied and broken, with here and there a cone like peak appearing—Glass Buttes to the south, Buck Mountain to the north, with Wagon Tire and Iron Mountains farther off. Early in the forenoon we had passed several homesteader's claims, spots of desolation in the desert, and now, as the afternoon wore on, the lonely settler's shack and wire fence began to appear again.

I have seen many sorts of desperation, but none like that of the men who attempt to make a home out of three hundred and twenty acres of High Desert sage. For this is so much more than they need. Three feet by six is land enough—and then there were no need of wire for a fence, or of a well for water. Going down to the sea in ships or into mines by a lift, are none too high prices to pay for life; but going out on the desert with a government claim, with the necessary plough, the necessary fence, the necessary years of residence, and other things made necessary by law, to say nothing of those required by nature and marriage, is to pay all too dearly for death, and to make of one's funeral a needlessly desolate thing. A man ploughing the sage—his woman keeping the shack—a patch of dust against the dust, a shadow within a shadow—sage and sand and space!

We are nearing Silver Creek, some forty miles, perhaps, from Burns, when ahead, and off to the right of us rose a little cloud of dust. I watched it with interest, wondering what it might be, until through the brush I made out a horseman galloping hard to intercept us, as I thought. I could not reach ahead with my eye to the windings of our narrow road, but unless we made in his direction we should leave him far in the rear. He had measured the distance , too, for I saw him bend in the saddle and the horse sink deeper into the sage as it lay down to the race. He was going to miss us surely, for we were driving like the wind. Then he snatched off his sombrero, waved it over his head, pulled hard right to take us farther down on a curve, and sent his horse at a dead run over a ridge of lava stones, a run to rob the rest of my automobile journey of all its terrors.

Our car slowed down, as the rider, a cowboy, lurched into the road.

"I've a dying man in here—" he began, jerking his hand toward a shanty off in the sage. "Will you take him to the doctor in Burns?"

The driver did not open his mouth, but turned and looked at us. The car was crowded; both running boards were piled with traps and luggage.

"He's dying of appendicitis," said the horseman. "An operation tonight might save him."

The gray of the evening had already spread over the desert, and at the ominous words it darkened till it touched the sage with a loneliness that was profound.

One of us would have to get off in the sage and give the dying man a place, and I, for every reason, was the one to do it. Must I confess that something like fear of that far circling horizon, of the deep silence, of the pall of gray sage and shadow took hold upon me! Dying? A man—yonder—alone?

Just then the second car, which we had passed some distance back, came up, and a long, lean man in a linen duster, who had eaten with me at the road house, hearing the story, hurried with us over to the shack.

"I'm a doctor," he said, leaving me unstrapping some luggage on the car, as he entered the door. He was out again in a minute.

"On the wrong side. Bad strain in the groin, that's all. He'll soon be in the saddle," and we were racing on toward Burns, the purring of the engine now a song of distances, of wide slumbering plains of sage and sand, and, overhead, of waking stars.

The long desert dusk still lingered, but lights were twinkling as we slowed through the last sandy ruts into the main street of Burns. We were met by the local game wardens and by some of the citizens of the town. Our talk was for tomorrow, Saturday, night. There was a "Booster Meeting" on for tonight. The next day I picked up on the street a little flyer.

TONIGHT
Tonawama Theatre
The Harney County Rod and Gun Club
Invites their friends to meet with them at
Tonawama Hall tonight at 8:30 to listen to
a talk by State Game Warden W.L. Finley,
who is accompanied here by Prof. Dallas Lor Sharp.
A special invitation is extended to the ladies.

Watch for Big Balloon Ascension Wednesday

The ladies came; the children, too. Not all of the thousand souls of Burns were out, for they had had the "Booster Meeting" the night before; but there was a considerable part of them out, to hear of the fish, the thirty thousand trout fry which were coming over the desert at the town's expense to stock the Silvies River and the creeks about Burns. I say at the town's expense; at the expense, rather of the Rod and Gun Club. But everybody belonged to the Rod and Gun Club. We had telegraphed our coming, and the gift of the fish, if the town would freight them in. The citizens got themselves together, raised the one hundred and twenty-five dollars, sent one of their men out with a five ton truck to meet us at Bend. But the fish train was delayed, and we had come on ahead, leaving the truck to follow when the fish should get in. By this time, however, they should have been in Burns.

Yes, we had seen their man. He had come through to Bend. And the fish? They had been sidetracked at The Dalles, but were on the road—had arrived at Bend, no doubt, at 9:45 last night, and must be now nearly in. Yes—they could certainly expect them by early morning, barring accidents—a fine lot of fingerlings, rainbows, silversides, and Eastern brook trout—forty cans of them!

It was an enthusiastic meeting in spite of the aired grievances of many of the Club against the tightening game laws, for which the warden was largely responsible. Enthusiastic, and decidedly enlightened too, it seemed to me, by the time it closed, and the warden had had a chance to explain the meaning of the relations between the sportsman, the game, and the State, and to enforce his points with that great load of young fish coming yonder over the desert.

"Finley," I said, after the meeting, "it's a long haul for fish."

"So it is," he replied.

"Suppose they don't arrive in good shape?"

"I was thinking of that; the long stop at The Dalles, to begin with; then this desert! They were shipped from the hatchery Friday. Tomorrow is Sunday. They'll never make it!"

We said no more. There was a good deal at stake for the game warden in this little town of Burns, the center of influence over a wider and a richer game country than can be found, I believe, anywhere else in the United States, fed as it is by the great Malheur Lake Reservation at the mouth of the Silvies, a few miles below.

At twelve o'clock that night I looked out into the sky. The stars were shining in the clear dark, and a strong wind was blowing cold from the desert. The truck had doubtless been on the road now for twenty-four hours. Where was it with its living freight, its forty cans of young fish, its two wardens, dipping, dipping all day, all night, to aerate the water and keep the fry alive? Those men had had no sleep all Friday night, none all day Saturday; they would get none tonight—all night. And the driver, the dusty, shock-headed driver who had met us at Bend! What did it mean to drive that heavy truck, with its perishing load, at top speed, without relief or sleep, over the tortuous trail and pulling sands of the High Desert clear to Burns! And all for a few thousand fish! They had been on the road for twenty-four hours. Should they arrive before morning there still could be no rest for the wardens, who must go from can to can dipping, dipping, dipping, till the fish were put into the streams!

At six o'clock the next morning, Sunday, we scanned the sagebrush to the west for a sign of the coming truck. There was no cloud of dust on the horizon. None at eight o'clock. None at ten. Noon came and went. Little groups of men gathered at the corners of the street or wandered in to talk with us at the "hotel." Buckboards and automobiles from distant ranches were waiting at the garage to take a can, or two cans, up and down the river twenty, thirty, forty miles away, when the truck should get in. The street was full of people—picturesque people, pure Americans all of them—"riders," homesteaders, ranchers, townspeople, waiting for the fish truck. The local baseball nines announced a game; the local band came out to escort them to the grounds, and, to the tune of "There'll be a Hot Time in the Old Town Tonight," went down to the field to play until the truck should come.

Four o'clock. I had ceased to look or care. My one hope now was that the truck would not get in, that it was a total wreck somewhere in the hopeless sagebrush of Crook County, where the road, I remembered, was next to impassable. They had mercifully had a break down, I was thinking, when there came a shout, a loud *chug-chugging*, and up to the hotel steps ground the truck, as grim an outfit as ever pulled in from a desert.

With the town a-trailing, the truck went on to the garage, where the water was quickly changed and iced down, the ranchers given their allotments of the young fish, and the unclaimed cans reloaded and hurried out to the nearest running stream.

But it was too late. I emptied the first can, and a little swirl of tiny whitish fish curled into an eddy and sank slowly to the bottom. One of them darted away—another keeled, curved out on its side, gasped, gulped the water, snapped himself into life at the taste, and swam weakly off—two out of eight hundred! It was so with every can.

We went back to the hotel. The driver of the truck, his clothes, hair, and skin caked with dust, his eyes bloodshot, and fearful exhaustion fastened upon his drawn face, dropped almost through my arms to a box on the sidewalk.

"Damn it!" he muttered, more to himself than to me, his arms limp, his head upon his knees, "they can pay me for the gas, and that's all they shall do."

But he got his pay for his time also. The game warden called the Rod and Gun Club together that night, and handed back a hundred dollars, saying the State would foot the bill this time. "You take the money," he said, "and we will build some hatching troughs in Cary Garden Creek with it tomorrow. I've telegraphed for fifty thousand trout eggs in the eyed stage—you can ship them in that stage round the world—and a warden to come with them to show you how they are hatched and planted. We will stock Silvies River and every stream about Burns, and do it now."

And so they did. In true Western style they started that hatchery the next day, and before the week had passed the work was done, the eggs were on the way, every man in the town interested, and every man won over to the side of the State in its fight for game protection and honest sport.

It is a great country, that Oregon country, as any one will say who makes the trip from Bend to Burns.

Chapter
VII **The Shadow
Of The Desert**

One of the principal reasons for Finley tak-
ing Sharp to Malheur Lake and marsh region was to follow up on reports of great
egrets in the area. These birds had been Finley and Bohlman's focal point in 1908
when the two men explored there. They were rewarded in 1912 by finding a small
colony at Silver Lake, a few miles from Harney and Malheur Lakes. (This Silver
Lake should not be confused with the town and lake also named Silver Lake, much
better known, and some 100 miles to the West, near Summer Lake.) It is interesting
that there was water in Silver Lake in 1912. Today it is generally thought of as always
having been an old dry lake bed.

The party stayed at the Double O Ranch, which is situated close to Silver Lake.
In a letter dated July 16, Sharp wrote his wife of the heron colony and the shooting
of a coyote.

Tuesday 5 am July 16, 1912
Dear Grace & Boys,

*Here I am 150 miles from a RR no matter which way I look, and here
the most remote spot left in the U.S., here is a woman and two little children—Wm & Winnie 5 & 3—and domestic life after its kind. Double O
Ranch is about 35 miles from Burns away off here 5 miles from Silver Lake
& I would say about 10 miles from Harney Lake (the latter in sight from
the rim rock behind the house which I just climbed) The nearest ranch is 5
miles away through the sage & alkali desert.*

*But you will want to know how we got to OO Ranch. Finley has hired a
big auto for the next few days (cost him $150 in hard cash) and yesterday
(Monday) we left Burns for Silver Lake—35 miles of wild sage desert with
only a wagon track to follow. Right over the rocks & brush we went, broke a
spring, 3 spark plugs, tail light etc., then out to the shores of the drying bitter
alkali lake and drive the car right across the hardened bed of the lake to a
point about a mile distant from the white heron colony—& 28 birds, the only
ones left in the West for which Finley has hunted there 12 years. He was
crazy of sight of them. He & I stripped, & with camera, field glasses & blind*

waded a long distance over to a great 1000 acre island where we could see the birds nesting in a clump of scrub willows. They were wild & flew—the old ones. We set up the blind & I went over the island to scare the old birds back. The island was a great camp ground for Indians & I hunted up 3 or 4 arrow heads of the black obsidian rock (lava glass).Off on one end of the island opposite the herons were about 300 pelicans resting in the water. It was mid afternoon by this time. We had seen two coyotes on the way & as the auto man & one of the wardens were lying under the car off across the water waiting for us a coyote came up and looked at them. They shot him with a revolver but though wounded he got away. We had left Jewett the collector & a warden back at an old shack a mile or two & when we returned he had prepared skins of sage rat, birds, & had killed & skinned a little rattlesnake. It was 7:30 by that time so we started off for OO Ranch, as they were expecting us & got here for supper at 8:30. It's now (6:30 after breakfast) and while Finley is photographing a baby sandhill crane hatched here under a hen I am sending you these hurried lines. The ride last night over the alkali desert in the evening light—miles & miles without a road, sometimes at 40 miles an hour was very strange, with jack rabbits jumping on every hand & the rim rock like some mighty walls low on the sky for miles & miles around. No words can picture the vastness, the wildness, the impossible character of this sagebrush & alkali land. This is the largest area in the US uncrossed by RR—the last of the real ranches. They are haying off some 3 or 4 miles (the ranch men) & we didn't see them roping & branding as they do that only in the spring & fall here. Here in the foremans quarters where we had good beds (only real sleep I've had since I left home) we found copies of Youth Companion with the Thanksgiving No. for 1911—but with the pages of the "Turkey Drive" torn out. All were disappointed. There is no glamour, no romance, no poetry about this life for me—except for the vastness of the plains. Life is little short of a nightmare as life in such a region—a woman's life lost past all hope. Out in the yard lies a dead unborn calf taken from a beef killed last week for the family. Big coyote hounds—6 of them—with only squalor & smells in & out of house & kids so dirty that as I saw them in their nighties I thought of the labor it would take to clean up their little mugs. (now we are off to the Silver Lake to our blind. I will finish later) ? later. We are stopping on the edge of a great dried up alkali lake that glares as white in the sun as this sheet of paper. Along the edge grows a scraggly "salt grass" that the jack rabbits seem to eat as we just saw a bunch of six jump out &

run. Their legs are all springs when they are really frightened—hopping high as if life were all a run and jump over the sage bunches xxxxxxxxxxxx

3:30 pm. Stopping at the red cabin after our return from the white heron colonies! Hot! Hot! Hot! The desert blisters and quivers in the heat. We are to start now back to Burns, where Finley meets the Rod & Gun Club tonight to give them a talk. I will mail this tonight so that it can start at 6am on that stage tomorrow. I don't know the program after tonight but it off toward the Steens Mts. & into them for a day or two.

I am sorry to leave you all so long. But you would die out here in this alkali desert, rich as it is distances rabbits & snakes. But try to keep in kindling & don't think of me as unmindful of you. I am not—not of one of the dear 5 of you. Now for 30 miles of thumpety-bump through the grease wood and sage.

Love to all & kisses. Dallas.

THE SHADOW OF THE DESERT

I saw the desert on the trip from Bend to Burns; I had some chance to watch it in the days that followed, as again by automobile we pushed far out over the gray wastes. We were bound for Silver Lake, off about thirty miles in the sage, where the wardens had discovered a small colony of American egrets (*Herodias egretta*). As we left the signs of trail and travel behind us and headed straight into the desert, I saw that we were in a wilder, barrener section than any we crossed on coming in from Bend. We were making the trip for white herons—egrets—but I began to feel coyotes about me in the sand and brush. I cannot explain just what the feeling of coyotes is, but I am sure you would have it out on the caked and crusty sand near Silver Lake. Everything said wolf as we sped silently along through the spaces of the sage. The lean, wide desert looked wolf. The deep silence spelled wolf. The black-tailed jacks jumped wolf as they flashed from the jaws of our own stalking car. And they ran as from wolves, when, over a smooth alkali bottom, we pushed up the throttle and sent the swift-footed machine hard at their heels. But it was the air, the aspect of things, rather, the sense of indescribable remoteness, withdrawal, and secrecy ever retreating before us, that seemed to take on form as something watchful, suspicious, inherently wild, something wolf-like. This was the wildest stretch of land, the most alien, that I had ever seen, and it must be here, if anywhere in the Northwest, that I should see the coyote, the desert wolf.

The creature's tracks were plain in the sand. He lurked behind every rise we topped, in every gully we cut, beyond every flat we crossed. By and by we fled through the caked and cracked bottom of some evaporated alkali lake, rounded a low rim rock into a green meadow, or coulee, and sighted the dull water of Silver Lake with its scalded shores bare and bleaching in the sun. A low edging of rock, the broken footings of a wall, ran around the shallow basin like a rude beading about some vast pewter salver. The thick water was rapidly shrinking. Off in the middle lay an island about a hundred acres in extent, at one end of which, on the surface of the lake, rested a great flock of white pelicans, and gleaming like flecks of snow against the green willow copse at the opposite end of the island perched a few white herons. The warden stood speechless at the sight of snow-white birds in the willows—they had been so nearly exterminated by the plumers—and his wonder fell upon us all.

We had left the car behind the wall of rock, allowing, for the first time, the absolute silence of the desert noon to come upon us. It was a new kind of silence to me, as utterly unlike any that I knew as the desert itself was unlike any stretch of my native landscape. One knows his silences as well, and listens as often to them, as one knows the voices of his birds, or the sounding tongues of stream, or storm, or forest, or shore. Even the drowsy quiet of an August noon over my Eastern fields differed from this dearth, this death of sound here in the desert, where the taut silence seemed drawn like shrunken skin over the bones of the sand and sage.

As we picked our way across the broken rock about the shore, a rattlesnake made the silence shiver; an avocet flew up with a note of woe, and then all was still again, the bones of cattle which lay scattered over the shallow valley quite as capable of stirring as any living thing in sight. Yet there was something stirring—yonder—a gray-brown shadow, far off on the alkali crust, a loping, backward looking figure which halts at the edge of the brush, then leaps the rocky rim and is lost—the coyote!

I stood staring after him when the automobile, having also

climbed the rocks, came up and whirled us over the flats to the distant side of the lake, where we were going to wade across to the egret colony on the island. I was soon in the water, stepping in the prints of the coyote which plainly showed beneath the surface, deep in the elastic, cement-like mud, and which led straight for the colony of the egrets. I was about halfway over, when a pistol shot rang out behind me and I turned in my tracks to see a coyote scurrying away from the automobile on three legs.

Doubtless it was the one that only a few minutes before I had seen disappearing in the sage and rabbit brush a mile away. He had followed us, had seen us well into the lake, and, thinking we all were gone, had trotted boldly out to inspect the car, the first automobile, I imagine, to penetrate to this desert haunt of his. But our driver was lying in the shade beneath the car, watching, and when the coyote came within easy range, fired at him, breaking his fore paw evidently, by the way it dangled as the poor beast spun about and dashed for the rocks.

He was a wolf, to be sure; but a wolf, if not an earth-born companion, is at least a fellow-mortal; and I turned again to following the clean, sharp footprints in the ooze, sorry for the dangling paw. It made no difference that the tracks led straight to the precious egret rookery, where they showed clearly enough what a scourge to the desert birdlife the creature must be. Lodged in a part of the willows was the body of a night heron, and underneath a great trampling of tracks. The carcass hung just out of the wolf's reach. A hundred times he had leaped for it, as no doubt, a hundred times he had crouched beneath the flimsy platforms in the matted willows, waiting for a nestling or an egg to fall. Out in the lupine and marginal grass we found a Canada goose nest, the nest of a Wilson's phalarope, and two or three mallards' nests which he had rifled. All of this was to the creature's discredit. I might heartily wish him dead; but I could not see him running maimed into the desert without pity and without protest against the careless shot.

You cannot follow the wild trails far without the conviction that the human hunter is the cruelest of all the beasts of prey. You will wonder if, for every creature killed, one has not got away wounded to die a dozen deaths in the brush. I am frequently coming upon the maimed and dying. Every woodsman and warden is reporting them.

Bohlman in camp

You cannot follow the sportsman far without foreseeing still longer closed seasons, much stricter regulations of all shooting, and even moral tests, and tests for marksmanship, before men with guns shall be allowed to go without official attendance into the woods. More than that, if you will follow the sportsman far enough, you will lose much of your taste for blood; you will be forced to the conviction that the pursuit of wild things no longer has its legitimate nor its most thrilling consummation in the kill. By the very nature of things there must be less killing, while, at the same time, there is bound to be an ever increasing multitude of those who love to hunt, and who may hunt but who must not kill; for there is a better way, without the chance of misery, and without the certain extinction that dogs the heels of the hunter as sure as his shadow. We are individually responsible, even while we put upon the State the burden for this better mind.

The driver of our car only laughed when I wondered how long the coyote with the broken leg might live. "He'll catch lizards and horned toads and picket-pins," said the man. "You needn't shed any tears over him. But the jacks will have the laugh on him all right."

As I watched the wind scoop and pile the sand about the butts of the sagebrushes, or saw the white drift scud and curl across the open; as I smelled the alkaloid vapors rising from the leprous lake, and felt the scurvy salt grass and the scabby crust crack under my feet, I could only marvel at life—that the sagebrush and the jack and the coyote could find a living in the wilds of this desert death. So far as I could discover, there was no live thing, not even algae, in the water of the lake; but here and there the rib of some starved steer, or a horn, protruding from the surface, as other bones, in whitened heaps, lay scattered about the shore. The white egrets and the pelicans crossed the desert to Harney and Malheur Lakes for their fishing. To find one's self with four good feet in a land like this were desperate enough; the odds are too many against the coyote with only three.

One would know by the head and face of the coyote that he is among the wisest and most capable of animals, schooled to privation and hardship, and able to hold his own, not only with the desert, but with the homesteader as well. He is doomed to disappear, utterly perhaps, for he is just enough larger than the fox and just enough more of a nuisance in a settled community to make himself the enemy of the farmer and the rancher who might overlook the smaller trespass of Reynard. Yet his presence seems needed upon the desert, for through a killer of poultry and lambs, and even of young calves, he is no such plague to the farmer as is the jack rabbit, whose only natural check, beside disease, he seems to be. The coyotes, a few years ago, were numerous about the town of Burns. We had gone thirty miles into the desert before seeing this one at Silver Lake. Left without their natural enemy, not only the jacks, but the little ground squirrels, or picket-pins, also, have so multiplied on the farms about the town as to become a plague. These squirrels are to be seen in the roads by half dozens; and I inspected one alfalfa meadow that was literally honeycombed with their tunnels, the crop so badly cut into that the damage could be seen at a glance. The farmer can more easily protect himself against the coyote than against the rabbit and the picket-pin.

This does not settle the problem of the coyote; and he is only one item in the very complicated and very serious problem of the unbalanced state of things everywhere in nature due to our taking over the affairs outdoors. That the sportsmen and game wardens hate him is natural. The loss of bird life in the ten mile range of a pair of hunting coyotes must be fearful, and when the ranges overlap, as usually they do, with two pairs or three pairs of the keen, hungry brutes quartering the territory, nothing but the nests out of reach in the trees can possibly escape. In the story of "The Coyote of Pelican Point" I have given an account of an exceptionally troublesome creature that preyed upon the bird colonies of Tule Lake southeast of the Klamath Lake Reservation, threatening the annihilation of the birds nesting in the grass about the shore and on the low lava rocks of a point that ran into the lake. The story is a story, the actual end of the creature not being as there recorded, but the havoc he wrought, and the difficulty experienced in trying to kill him, his cunning and craft when traps were set for him, and dogs sent after him, are in no wise colored, the facts having been given to me as there put down. This fellow lay in the lap of luxury, the abundant wading birds of the lake, such as stilts and killdeer, and those swimmers, like the ducks and geese, that build in the marginal grass, being his easy prey; the gulls and other swimmers, such as terns and pelicans and cormorants, escaping him, in most part, by treading down the tule

Sharp and wardens at Silver Lake

islands in the middle of the lake and on these rearing their young.

But it takes the wide prairie, or the desert, to bring out the best in the coyote. He is the hunter of the plains, the rich grass or stunted sage or scattered rocks hiding him equally well, and yielding him his meager but sufficient meat. Fitted for the plains, he lives where almost any other carnivore would die, combining in himself the physical and mental characteristics of both fox and wolf. Sagacity and endurance mark him, and a peculiar ingenuousness, inquisitiveness perhaps, that leaves his face without a trace of savagery. He is pretty nearly a dog, and in fact is the one member of his wild tribe that has a well developed bark. And, like the dog, he loves to bark, the dusk and moonlight filling his soul with a solemn music that every sojourner on the plains has listened to. No more weird or haunting note was ever heard, eerie, wistful, melancholy, as if the inarticulate tongue would utter things unutterable, dim brute desires that our human tongues long since have clothed with words. I have never seen the timber wolf at home, nor ever heard his "hunting song," but those who have tell me that it is one of the fearful sounds of the forest, sinister and savage. The little red fox that trots across my fields daily, and that frequently "barks" outside my window, has a voice as wild as the wolf's, a raucous, raw, uncultivated, untrained yap which I doubt if even the dogs of the neighboring farms recognize as belonging to one of their tribe, so indescribably alien does it sound, breaking in upon the faint puff, puff of the engine off beyond the woods, or the muffled passing of an automobile on the distant highway, or the murmur of church bells rising and falling over the fields. The coyote is more wolf than fox, but more dog than wolf, and his lonesome baying beneath the desert moon, so strangely touched with sentiment, so filled with longing, would blend better with the human sounds of my twilight than it does with the savage silence of the plains. It is a brute voice, but so nearly human, as it calls to me across the sage and shadows, that I could answer and, it seems, be almost understood.

The coyote became a denizen of the desert, no doubt, by necessity, the larger gray wolf, whose tastes and habits were similar, taking the better stocked timber and bottom lands and forcing the coyote into the open prairie and the sage plains to make whatever shift he might. He has been equal to it, the hardness of his desert life, I like to think, making a better wolf out of him. I say wolf, and the better the wolf the more we may hate him. But one cannot help admiring many of his ways and traits.

The exigencies of desert life have made mutual help and team work necessary among the coyotes, two of them hunting together more successfully than one, a fact that perhaps explains their mating and staying together from year to year. It is generally supposed that coyotes mate for life, the pair appropriating an old badger's burrow, or even digging one of their own, and then, with squatter's rights, taking for their own hunting grounds enough each way from their den to support them. These haunts, of course, overlap, two or three pairs sometimes getting together in a hunt; but generally the coyote works alone, or in single pairs, each pair's own range being apparently respected by the near neighbors.

There are few chapters of natural history more interesting than those describing the team and relay hunting of the coyote, especially when antelope are the game. Dr. L.E. Hibbard, of Burns, an authority on the wild life of the desert, told me of a hunt of coyotes that he had a hand in, which illustrates not only the cunning of the hunters, but the remarkable love and courage of the mother antelope as well.

Dr. Hibbard was in the desert for young antelope and had been scouring the sage for hours, when, coming up to the edge of a sharp rim rock that dropped into a flat, he looked down upon the thick sage and saw an old doe antelope with three young ones which was trying to hide. The kids seemed to be about two weeks old—old enough to be able to run with the mother, but for some reason she was anxiously trying to conceal them. Then he saw that one of the three was lame and could not run, that this one was perhaps not the mother's own at all, but a motherless cripple that had adopted her or that she had adopted and was trying to rear. Her own two (if these two were hers) could have followed her; it was on account of the cripple that she was trying to hide them. But they did not wish to hide. They were too old. Speed had already come to their winged legs, and speed was the very breath of their young lives. Yet they must hide. She would stop and nurse them—all three of them—and lie down with them until they would separate and get out of sight under the sage, or more generally on a floe of rock similar in color to themselves; then, teetering, peeking, spying behind her, she would edge quietly away, and steal off just like a poorly trained human mother tiptoeing out of a room from her sleeping child. She would not get far before up would come their little ears, then their noses, then up they would jump and make after her.

Again she would lead them on until she found a good hiding place, then down they would go, the whole sleeping child performance gone through with again, to be spoiled again by the restless little kids hopping out of their beds and calling "Mamma!" Over and over mamma tried to hide them, moving off the flat in her effort, and down a narrow valley, the watcher on the rim rock following her quite unobserved.

The repeated attempts had taken the antelope several miles down the valley to where it opened out into a wide sage flat. She had led them on for perhaps a mile, when, coming to a dense patch of rabbit brush, she put them to bed again, this time successfully, for immediately her legs began to twinkle as, whisking past the hunter, hidden in a low juniper some distance out in the flat, she made off up the valley.

Marking the spot where the young were hidden, Dr. Hibbard was climbing down toward them, when he heard a sharp blat and saw the three young antelope tearing down the trail toward him, the lame one falling a little behind. At the same time he saw the old antelope, her hair puffed, racing at top speed back toward him and the coming young ones and, down a parallel trail through the sage, running neck and neck with the mother, three coyotes, who had evidently been watching the whole affair from the edge of the rim rock.

It was a race between the mother and the coyotes to reach the young ones first, though she kept just in front of the wolves as if to keep them back from the kids. But the coyotes were at her heels, and as they neared the kids, one of the three brutes, outrunning the others, came up at her side and, cutting in ahead, leaped for one of the little fawns. He seized it by the neck, but as he did so he received a terrific shoulder stroke from the mother, who, with a twist in midair, leaped at him as he leaped at the kid. It rolled over and over, flashed to its feet without ceasing its forward motion, and was off, while the mother, quick after the shoulder blow, fetched the coyote a racking dig in the ribs with all four of her sharp hoofs that sent him spinning and snapping heels over head in the sage.

Then the race for life was on again. The doe, now leaving two of the kids to their wits and their heels, hung at the side of the crippled one, which the wolf had attacked. The coyote was with her, watching for an opening; but her defense was marvelous, she and the kid seemed one, as hawk and sparrow seem one zigzagging through the air. She literally covered him as they darted along. But the little fellow's strength was failing. Suddenly the wolf whipped under the flank of the mother and with a long leap again caught the kid by the throat, only again to get the terrific shoulder blow and the raking broadside from her knife-like hoofs. She had forced him to drop his prey the second time, the kid never losing an instant in getting to his feet and running on.

But he staggered now. The chase had been going in a wide circle, bringing the runners around somewhere near their staring place, and near to the two coyotes that had fallen behind, who, fresh from the fray, started in with their companion to finish the work. Meanwhile the two other young antelopes had run off and hid—flat to the ground somewhere, the invisible cap drawn over them, the odorless wind blowing across them—where the keen-eyed, keen-nosed coyote would have to step upon them before he could discover that they were not stones on the desert sand.

The race was almost over, however, for the little handicapped one, the mother bravely beating off the wolf in her desperate fight to save the bleeding, tottering thing. The coyote was still afraid of her shoulder and her terrible hoofs, but now merely dodged her strokes, growing bolder as the kid came tottering to his knees, when again he leaped and seized it.

At this point the companion of Dr. Hibbard came shouting up and prevented the doe from again attacking the wolf, which, hoping to escape from the man, held his prey and flattened himself to the sand. But the hunter rushed at him with stones, and the coyote, dropping the kid, ran into the sage. The other two coyotes now joined him, circling about the man, who was without a gun, as they tried to find the little antelope. But he finally drove them off. The poor little kid, however, was dead, its throat torn by the fierce fangs that the mother repeatedly had broken from their fatal hold.

But the other two kids escaped—only to fall later, perhaps to the same fangs. It was a close call—as it will be the next time, as it always is on the desert and here in my own Eastern woodlot, and elsewhere, everywhere. I did not see an antelope in these deserts, though I traveled hundreds of miles looking for them. I had to content myself with studying a tame one at the Narrows, that had been captured in the sage. Yet a few months after my trip through the plains, the State's wardens counted several hundred antelope where I thought they must have become extinct. The coyote and they have always dwelt together on the desert, the hand of Nature giving differently, but giving evenly, to them both.

There used to be no shadow on the desert. Death crossed; but only Life dwelt among the rim rocks and the sage. The gray-brown shadow that I had seen on the shores of Silver Lake was no shadow at all; it was a coyote. But that evening as we left Silver Lake behind us and were speeding out through the sage, we came upon a straight, interminable line of squared pine stakes set low in the sand, the trail of the surveyor driven into the breast of the desert; and a long, interminable line of stakes cast a long, interminable shadow—the shadow of a coming railroad that lay direct and dark across the plain.

Chapter
VIII On The Marshes Of Malheur

Today the Narrows is just one small ranch. There certainly isn't anything left which would indicate a town the size of which Sharp wrote on July 18th. In fact, looking at the Narrows today one wonders just where all the buildings were? From this point the party put out into vast Malheur Lake and its nearly endless marshes. Then, as today, it was wonderfully rich with bird life.

Of special interest in this chapter is the very large eared grebe colony the party found. This striking little bird was also shot for its feathers, but most of the grebe killing took place on Klamath Marshes. Today about eight hundred pairs nest on Malheur Refuge. But in 1979 twelve hundred pairs nested on west Harney Lake. However, this is still far short of the remarkable 2,465 nests counted by Finley's warden in 1912.

July 18, 1912. At Narrows Hotel, The Narrows. 3 saloons, 2 hotels, grocery store & black smith shop abuilding. The Narrows is a neck between Malheur & Harney Lakes. Harney is so alkali & bitter that no bird life or fish can live in it. Malheur is brimming with life. We are now off to Malheur to see a grebe colony of 24 hundred nests anchored to tule & weeds right out in open water. A tame antelope is running about the yard but is soon to die as he has reached his 2nd birthday & they die within 2 or 3 weeks (usually in captivity) of the 2nd year. Life is arid here in the wild sagebrush land. From here to Burns over Wrights Point is about 25 miles. A wide view of Harney Valley lies open under one on top of the narrow ridge of Wrights Point; with Silvies River a green window in a green meadow. Then we descend into level sagebrush & ride through the sand, past miles of homesteads cutting around their corners in order to avoid crossing their fenced in claims. Jacks, burrowing owls, sage thrashers, here & there a foraging bull, the blue desert lily on its slender stem & leaves dried & curled into a string of tendrils into large patches of glowing white fragrant evening primrose equal to the ground swell is everywhere. It was cloudy (a rare day in this part) & the shining & white & honey sweet flower of the gilia was along the road. Started from Narrows 6:45 & over the miles of sagebrush to Buena Vista Range 20 miles. M. gulch 15 m. out we killed R snake. He was back in a hollow under the lava sandstone, & when 10 feet away began his rattle. He had only 3 rattles.

ON THE MARSHES OF MALHEUR

The sedges were full of birds, the waters were full of birds, the tules were full of birds, the skies were full of birds: avocets, stilts, willets, killdeer, coots, phalaropes, rails, tule wrens, yellow-headed blackbirds, black terns, Forster's terns, canvasback, redhead and ruddy ducks, Canada geese, night herons, great blue herons, Farallon cormorants, great white pelicans, great glossy ibises, California gulls, eared grebes, Western grebes—clouds of them, acres of them, square miles—one hundred and forty-three square miles of them!

Dallas Jr. with double-crested cormorant

I was beside myself at the sight—at the sound—at the thought that such wild life could still be anywhere upon the face of the earth, to say nothing of finding it within the borders of my own land. Here was a page out of the early history of our country; no, an actual area of that wild, unspoiled, unslaughtered country as the Indian knew it, as Lewis and Clark saw it on that first trip across the continent.

The accounts of bird-life in early American writings read to us now like the wildest of wild tales—the air black with flocks of red-winged blackbirds, the marshes white with feeding herons, the woods weighted with roosting pigeons. I have heard my mother tell of being out in a flock of passenger pigeons so vast that the sun was darkened, the birds flying so low that men knocked them down with sticks. As a child I once saw the Maurice River meadows white with egrets, and across the skies of the marshes farther down, unbroken lines of flocking blackbirds that touched opposite sides of the horizon.

That was years ago. I had seen nothing like it since; nor did I ever again expect to see it. I had heard of Malheur Lake, when, some few years ago, the naturalist through whose efforts it was made Federal reservation visited me and told me about it. He even brought photographs of its bird colonies. But words and pictures gave no conception of the extent of its uncrowded crowds of life. For what could a camera do with one hundred and forty-three square miles of swimming, winging, crying birds?

Malheur Lake Reservation is in the southeastern quarter of Oregon, and is only one of several such wild life sanctuaries within the borders of that great commonwealth. Indeed, the work being done by Oregon for the protection of wild life seems almost past belief to one used to the small things of the Eastern States. And the work there has but just begun! In 1912 the private game "refuges" where the State Game Warden has entered into contracts with owners of private land, covered an area of 143,789 acres. In addition to these small refuges there are six vast state reservations, set aside forever by the Legislature for game and bird protection, covering 1,698,320 acres, or 2,654 square miles, an area more than twice the size of Rhode Island. Beside these state reservations are the four great Federal preserves: Three Arch Rocks Reservation, off the coast; Klamath Lake Reservation, lying partly in Oregon and partly in California; Cold Springs Reservation, in Umatilla County, in the northeast; and Malheur Lake Reservation, including the waters and marshlands of Malheur and Harney Lakes, and situated in the midst of protecting sagebrush plains that stretch from the foothills of the Cascades eastward to the canon of the Snake River at the foot of the Rockies in Idaho.

Separated thus by the deserts from any close encroachment, saved to itself by its own vast size and undrainable, unusable bottoms, and guarded by its Federal warden and the scattered ranchers who begin to see its meaning, Malheur Lake Reservation must supply waterfowl enough to restock forever the whole Pacific slope.

For here in the marsh of burr reed and tule, the wild fowl breed as in former times when only the canoe of the Indian plied the lake's shallow waters, when only the wolf and the coyote prowled about its wide, sedgy shores. I saw the coyote still slinking through the sage and salt grass along its borders; I picked up the black obsidian arrowheads in the crusty sand on the edge of the sage plain; and in a canoe I slipped through the green walled channels of the Blitzen River out into the sea of tule islands amid such a flapping, splashing, clacking, honking multitude as must have risen from the water when the red man's paddle first broke its even surface.

No, not quite such a multitude, for there was no snowy gleaming of egrets in the throngs over head. The plume hunter had been before us, and the glory of the lake was gone. That story is one of the tragedies of bird life, and vividly told in William L. Finley's account of "The Trail of the Plume-Hunter," in the *Atlantic Monthly* for September, 1910. He says, writing of his and Bohlman's journey into the Malheur country in 1908:

"We had hunted where one might think no human being had ever been, but long before we had traveled over these apparently unknown regions, plumers had preceded us. We followed in their trails. We camped where they had camped. We had traveled hundreds of miles exploring the haunts where white herons used to live, but up to the summer of 1908 we had not seen a single one of these birds.

"This is historic ground for the bird man. In the early seventies the well known ornithologist, the late Captain Charles Bendire, was stationed at Camp Harney on the southern slope of the Blue Mountains, straight across the valley from where we stood. He gave us the first account of the bird life in this region. He saw wonderful sights of the nesting multitudes. He told of the colonies of white herons that lived in the willows along the lower Silvies River. There was the river itself winding across the valley through sage, rye grass flats, and tule marshes, its trail marked by a growth of willow and alder.

"Two days ago we had followed this trail, and searched out these places to photograph the white heron. As we approached the trees, said to be alive with birds, all was silent.

"We're on the wrong trail again," my companion had suggested; but pushing through the willows I saw big nests in the trees on both sides of the river. Strange to say, not a single bird! I clambered up to one of the lower nests, and found a rough platform of sticks upon which lay the bleached bones of two herons. I climbed another and another. Each home was a funeral pyre.

"Epidemic?" said my companion.

"Yes, of plume hunters!" I retorted.

"Here was a great cemetery in the silence of the marsh. But one nest was inhabited. A long-eared owl was in possession sitting on five eggs. As we approached, she spread her wings, and left without a sound. Ill-omened creature brooding eggs and bones!

"Standing here high above the valley, with my field glass I picked out the very spot of this great bird massacre that we had visited.

"I hope we find no more like that,' said my companion as he tightened the camera straps about his shoulders, and started off down the trail toward the lake.

"We were both confident that somewhere down in that distant sea of green tules, we could find at least one place where white herons were nesting.

"We outfitted for a week's trip, and set out down the spring branch. This time we kept a straight course to the north until we reached the main body of the lake. All day long we hunted and watched the birds, lining them with our field glasses as they flew back and forth over the lake. We saw no signs of white herons.

"That day we found a colony where the great blue heron nested. White herons were formerly common here, both species nesting together. Not a single white bird left!

Sharp in the marsh with wardens

"We spent the next four days here and there through the vast extent of tule islands and water, searching and keeping watch all day, trying to find white herons. Late one afternoon we came to a place where another big colony of blue herons was nesting. We had been seeking this place. Malheur Lake is divided in several parts by the long lines of tule islands. We were in the northern part. The colony was on two long tule islands that lined up with Pine Knob and the east end of Wright's Point. On the north end is a big canebrake.

"We sat in the boat at the edge of the canebrake, and watched the big birds as they sailed over, dropping in, and departed. We were tired from the long day's search. I did not then know the story as I know it now: but hidden in the end of this canebrake a hunter had had his blind, ten years before.

"That summer of 1898 was eventful in white heron history here on Malheur Lake. Early in the season two men had arrived at Narrows, bought lumber, and built a flat-bottom, double-ended boat. They set out from Narrows with a small outfit. They fought mosquitoes day and night as we had; they drank the alkali water; they slept in the boat or on muskrat houses while they hunted up and down the waters of the lake and the tule islands. They saw the great flocks of white pelicans, cormorants, terns, gulls, grebes, and other birds. They saw the white herons in slow, stately flight wherever they went, but it was not till after several days that they located the big colony here on the island by the canebrake, the greatest colony they had ever seen. What a sight it must have been, thousands of these birds, dazzling white in the sun, coming and going from the feeding grounds, and hovering over their homes!

"On all sides were the homes, built up a foot or two from the surface, each having three or four frowsy-headed youngsters or as many eggs. At each end of the colony a plumer sat hidden in his blind. At the first crack of the gun, a great snowy bird tumbled headlong near its own nest. As the shot echoed across the lake, it sounded the doom of the heron colony. Terror-stricken, on every side white wings flapped, till the air was completely filled. Shot followed shot unremittingly as the minutes passed into hours. Still the heron mothers came to hover over this scene of death and destruction. Mother love was but the lure to slaughter.

"By two o'clock in the afternoon, the day's shoot ended. It took the rest of the day for the hunters to collect the dead and take the plumes. Stripping the plumes is rapid work. It takes but the slash of the knife across the middle of the back, a cut down each side, and a swift jerk.

"Long after dark the plumers heard the steady quacking clatter of young herons crying to be fed. Far into the night, hoarse croaks sounded over the still lake, greetings of those birds that had spent the day fishing in distant swamps. It argued good shooting again for the morrow.

"The second day was a repetition of the first. Heron numbers thinned rapidly. Here on these two islands, the plumers harvested a crop that yielded twelve hundred dollars in a day and a half. They collected a load of plumes worth their weight in gold. Were the California days of '49 much better?

"Malheur has seen many such massacres, but none so great as that. Little did we know of these facts as we sat watching the blue herons coming and going, expecting to find at least a few white herons somewhere about the locality.

"After hunting for seven days we returned to camp for more provisions, and set out to visit another part of the lake. This time we stayed out for nine days, and saw—two white herons! At the time we thought these must be part of a group that nested somewhere about the lake; yet more likely they were a single stray bird that came our way twice. I am satisfied that of the thousands of white herons formerly nesting on Malheur, not a single pair is left."

It may have been two birds that they saw and not one. For he has not told all of the story yet; how in the summer of 1912 he received a telegram saying white herons (the American egret) had been seen passing over the marshes of Malheur; nor how we set off from Portland for Burns; nor how, away off on an island in the alkali water of Silver Lake, some fifty miles in the desert from Malheur, we found the birds—a colony of a dozen pairs, numbering with the young about twenty-eight birds all told; nor how—

But that is for him to tell, if he will. For if the egret is ever again seen flying over the inland waters of the Pacific coast, it will be due to William L. Finley, to his discovery of the slaughter on his trip into the Malheur in 1908, and to his efforts which made Malheur a wild bird reservation...

But was it, we wonder, one bird or two that he saw winging over the lake in 1908? If two birds, were they male and female? And were they the last two? And is this small colony which we discovered four years later in Silver Lake, the seed of that last solitary pair? Could it have been that the race was so nearly cut off in all this part of the world? And does it mean that slowly now, with the new protection of these better times, the egret will come back to the willows along the Silvies and at Clear Lake, and to the islands in the canebrake of the Malheur?

I think so. In the willows of Silver Lake, I counted twenty-eight birds. These are enough if they are given a chance. The life of the species, however, does not hang upon this perilously slender thread. Along the Gulf and Southern Atlantic States, and in the Middle West, small colonies are reported as surviving, mere handfuls, where the plume hunter found immense rookeries. Bird lovers the world over are watching these remnants with intense concern. Nowhere were the herons as nearly wiped out, it appears, as in Oregon; and nowhere

Dallas Lore Sharp

will their escape and ultimate restoration seem more of a miracle.

While here on Malheur I witnessed a sight among the grebes, that gave me further reason for my faith in the resources of Nature, open as the happening may be to a contrary interpretation.

On the day of our arrival at the town of Burns the wardens of Malheur met us with the report of a new grebe colony (these birds had also nearly been exterminated by the plume hunter), which they had discovered only the day before off in the lake. We had ridden across the desert that afternoon in the teeth of a stiff wind, and the wardens, anxious to show us the new colony, were greatly concerned for fear that this wind might wreck the nests exposed to its sweep across the wide level of the lake.

For it was nesting time and the colony had built far out on the open water in a close, continuous line a mile long and three hundred yards wide—a community of twenty-four hundred floating nests.

The figures are true. The wardens actually staked off the colony, measured it, and literally counted the nests. I paddled along its length myself, and while I did not count, I did believe their figures.

It was to visit this colony of grebes that we wound our way through the narrow turnings of the Blitzen River out into the wider maze of the vast lake, where there was nothing to be seen but water and tules—and birds, myriads of birds. But the wardens had blazed a trail by tying the tule tops together into big knots, which we could see from island to island ahead of us as we paddled along.

This was on Monday. It was on Thursday the week before that the wardens had found the colony; and now, as we came out of the mouth of the Blitzen, we ran straight into a grebe colony of over a hundred nests that was not there at all four days before. One of the wardens, who was in the canoe with us, thought we must be off the course. But here were his knots in the tules. The nests had been built, all of them, since Thursday, and most of them were already with eggs.

There must be some mistake, I thought, and turned to watching the birds; for it was not the nests that interested me half so much as the anxiety of the grebes at discovering us. Every one began hurriedly pulling the wet tule stems and milfoil of the nest over her eggs to hide them before we should come up, working against her fears, and at the risk of her life, to save her eggs—to protect the seed of the race!

The grebe builds a floating nest out in the open water. All over the bottom of the clear lake, which averaged about four feet in depth, grew the long, trailing, moss-like water-milfoil, its whorled leaves and purple stems giving a faint glow of color to the water as we looked down into it. The grebes dive to the bottom and drag up this milfoil into heaps, or cocks, about six feet across on the bottom. The cocks are barely able to float their tops above the surface. Upon the very peak of this cock they hollow out a nest about the size of a man's hat, building up the walls with dead tule stems until the eggs rest just out of the water, though many of them are partly submerged. The nests are usually so close together that their wide bases touch below, but otherwise they are entirely unanchored and at the mercy of wind and wave.

This was the cause of the warden's anxiety, and, halting only long enough to count the new nests and get some photographs at the mouth of the river, we pushed on up the lake.

I shall try to describe that trip sometime—the long lines of white water kicked up by the rising birds; the clapping of wings, the splashing of feet; the tule islands trodden flat by the rookeries of young gulls and pelicans and cormorants; the diving of the grebes about us; the soaring of the majestic pelicans far above us—but not any of that now.

We had paddled for an hour or two when on the water in the distance appeared a wide wash of pink, as if the clouds of a sunset were reflected there. It was the purple of the milfoil in the nests of the great grebe colony. We quickened our stroke, and as we drew nearer, marveling at the extent of it, we were struck with the silence at our coming and the absence of birds in the nests. A few were on wing; a few were seen covering their eggs; that was all. There was no clangor of the crowd, no diving multitude about us—but such a sight of destruction as I hope never again to see!

Of the twenty-four hundred nests not three hundred were left. Tossed and torn, the nests had been driven by the high waves and the strong wind back upon themselves, in some places several deep, their pale white eggs by thousands scattered through the tangled debris or floating free in the water.

The rookery was an utter wreck. The birds, with the exception of a few pairs, had abandoned it—had gone, some hundred pairs of them, down to the mouth of the Blitzen and there started the new colony which we had encountered coming out.

I don't know which impressed me more—the fearful loss and waste of life here, or the thought of that quick recovery at the mouth of the Blitzen.

The birds had shown no judgment in choosing this place for their rookery. No more exposed position could have been found in the entire lake. The colony had acted blindly, stupidly; had learned nothing as a colony in their million ages of nest building, nor ever shall learn. But how swift to begin again! How fertile in resource! How absolute to command! With the nest done, the season's clutch of eggs lain, and incubation started, to see it all destroyed, and in less than a week to have built again and to have summoned the secret forces of life with new eggs for the new nests!

A bare handful of the former myriads of the white herons, or egrets, are left on Malheur. I hope to make the trip again from Bend to Burns, and from Burns down to Malheur Reservation, in order to see the gleaming, shimmering flocks of the snowy creatures that I am sure shall be passing to and from their island rookeries in the cane and tules at the head of the marshy lake.

The Spirit Of The Herd

After Malheur the Finley/Sharp party traveled down the Blitzen valley to Peter French's old ranch—the P Ranch. Here they spent a night, and then climbed up on Steens Mountain for an overnight trip. Finley, in part, went to check whether any of the bighorn sheep once common in the region were left. From that point they crossed over into the Catlow Valley. They visited both Roaring Springs Ranch and Home Creek Ranch, the latter likely not looking much different today than when Finley/Sharp visited, or during the Indian attacks on the ranch about 30 years before.

They then took the old army trail out of the Catlow Valley across the desert to the Warner Valley, and the town of Plush. On July 23rd they traveled to Lakeview, then back to Bend. In total, they had made a great circuit through the heart of Oregon's Great Basin.

During this time frame Sharp wrote two letters which have been saved. Of great interest is the first, dated July 19th, and written while at the P Ranch. He mentioned that the foreman of the ranch told him of a stampede which took place some years before as they were driving the cattle down to the railhead at Winnemucca, Nevada. From that account Sharp formed his *The Spirit Of The Herd* chapter.

P RANCH, 200 miles from RR,
17 days drive for the herds to RR, 40 miles from Burns
July 19, 1912

Dear Grace and Boys
I am writing to you in the main room of the main or White House of P Ranch with the general overseer & all our gang sitting about smoking & talking. We came down the Blitzen River valley 40 miles & all the way were on this ranch. North & South this single property is 75 miles long— the largest ranch in Oregon, if not the largest in the U.S. Off from the west are hills. The ranch with its very tall sombordy poplars and middle west cotton woods in rows all around, looks like some Italian villa, or as if might be an old Feudal castle. As you come in through enormous gate, with the multitude of stockade coralls (pens!) and the many sheds, barns & storage

buildings, together with the "bunkhouse", the store, the cookhouse, the office, this "White House" & the big blacksmith shops make a group in a setting positively new and picturesque. Such poplars you never saw. They are planted for fences along the fences around the houses. They were planted about 35 years ago & are now about 90 to 100 feet in height and slender as a pole. The tallest slenderous trees I ever saw for non-forest trees. There are about 35,000 head of cattle all told. Last fall & spring they sold 8,000 head and drove them off of the Mts & valleys nearly 200 miles to Winnemucca to the Southern Pacific RR—17 days of driving! The stockade corals (pens) are all made of the trunks of Juniper trees which grow up on the Mt sides—away off from here, set into the ground and tied together with rawhide for rawhide was once much cheaper than wire! The rawhide is green & has the hair on when the inch wide thongs are bound on, then it hardens and shrinks till it ties like iron. Remember there are no trees in this country— they burn the sagebrush, so that all lumber is brought in from Bend etc.—200 & more miles away by team! Great home made gates swing everywhere from whole Juniper trees for posts—very interesting & effective. I can't begin to tell you about the "Round Barn"—like an enormous open umbrella inside where they "break" ponies in the winter, nor about the shambles where they slaughtered a beef tonight, nor about the roping corals (spelling!!), nor the branding, nor the "separating shute" through which the herds are driven to separate heifers & steers etc etc. too long! Finley has taken pictures—they will show.

Our trip today from The Narrows (natives call it "na (gnar) nous)— was through the desert again, but we climbed high up over the bench land up two or three heights of laval rim rock where miles & miles of grey grey-land with frowning rim rock all around lay—around us—impossible, unconquered & unconquerable. Then we descended into Blitzen valley & for miles came on down to the Ranch. We killed a big rattler on the way, shot two ravens & one beautiful striped ground squirrel as large as a small woodchuck. Tomorrow we take a wagon & horses and ascend the Steins Mts. (pronounced Steens) for 14 miles, then on foot to the still snow blotched peaks for a look down Blitzen gorge. We will camp up there all night & get down for a trip into Catlow Valley Sunday at the Home Ranch.

After leaving Narrows & some miles of sage brush behind we began to see Jackass Mt, but did not have to climb it as the water on the meadows was off & allowed to run down the "draws" or valley-like—between the *rimrock—volcanic sand stone & basalt (breaking in its typical columnar form). Rim rock is the rock at the edge of the high level plateaus (spelling!) or table lands left after the erosion that has sent the laval sands etc into the valleys & deserts.*

On our way down we stopped at Buena Vista Ranch to see the Indian writings (lizards, men, turtles etc) on a smooth face of sandstone.

Now it is bedtime & I will stop this—to continue tomorrow. I think of you in Oregon with me; but I am separated tonight from you a day longer farther than I would be in N.Y. City! It will take this (or me) longer, if started on its way back to you to reach Jennings Lodge than I would if started tonight for NY City.—even with the Auto! Oh yes, before I stop: The boss of the Buckaroos (cowboys) has gone all over in detail a tip top story for me—we sat out on the bridge (over the Blitzen) in front of the ranch & he gave me all the details of a stampede story! A good days work for me! So dear ones, goodnight and may God bless us—you bless each of you Mother, Mansie, Beetum, Betsie baby & father—all. Love & Love & love—good night. Father & Dallas.

P Ranch to Plush, July 22, 1912

I am writing by candle light on a trunk out in a hall at Plush Hotel—no chair in room! Of all the trips by auto—the worst & most interesting—up the rim rock & down into Catlow Valley—on to Plucke's sheep ranch for dinner & into a nameless rock sage land with a climb climb climb to the base of Warner Mts., then up Mts and down the most fearful road to Warner Lake—then by Flag Pole Lake through alkali flats to the high road into these 2 hotels, general store & ranch place. A cold wind & rain storm struck us in Catlow Valley, we dried out at Roaring Springs Ranch, then came on into sunshine & a desert of hop toads. The road and land were all a-hop with them—all of them going before us up the ruts like sheep. We were miles from water, but out of the earth they had come for their welcome drink, for a red ant out (we opened several stomachs) to grub then while we were watching them back into the soil—as if the "plague" had seen Aaron's wand, and disappeared. While we watched the innumerable hosts vanished, 2 or 3 together sometimes, backing in out of sight away down in the sanding soil to wait (I wonder) for the next rain? Where do they breed? How long would the red ant or two last them? They were full of water.

We turned over stones and caught a number of scorpions—big & little. Very abundant. Saw many sage hens—they got up with loose rattle of wings, flying & skimming with a sidewise veer—like a quail.

July 23, 1912

From Plush to Lakeview 44 miles—down the Warner canyon among the great pines with their reddish cones, big lined yellow red trunks, but oh! the sheeped off slopes with their parallel lines. We descended Warner Lake rim, the most perilous grade off Warner Mt, I ever made in car. No auto has been known to ascend it.

July 24, 1912

We left Lakeview at 7:20 am and eating out of hand along the road drove all day to Bend—200 miles. It was a trip largely through hills, some deep ravines & descents, some hard climbs up,, all the way much varied & for miles through the great open yellow pine forests, roomy, spacious clean & grand. Chipmunks, ground squirrels, Steller's jays, here & there a great horned owl, Cooper's hawk, & the western tanager. We passed through 2 great forest reservations, through several tracts of white (western) & lodge pole pines. Outside of LaPine a tire blew up & got us 1 ? hours late into Bend. Lewis woodpeckers abound here.

THE SPIRIT OF THE HERD

None of our domestic animals is milder-eyed or of a meeker mien than the cow. She is never abject like the donkey; but centuries of gentling and giving down have made her cowlike, until she is in danger of forever losing her horns. She is not in any danger of forgetting how to use horns, however. More than once have I been chased in the evening by the cow I had driven peacefully to pasture in the morning. On one occasion I narrowly escaped with my life from the kindest of old cows, one which I had been driving to the meadows all summer. Her newborn calf was the trouble. She had hidden it among the mallows, stationed herself near by and waited for me, as a thousand years before she had waited for the wolf or the bear. Her swift and unexpected lunge was the very fury of wildness.

Little as domestication has changed the individual animal, it has changed still less the animal group—the herd, the flock, the pack. The spirit of the pack and herd spring from deep and primal needs—common fear, or hunger, or the call of kind to kind. The gregarious animal must be separated from its clan to be domesticated. Allowed to return to the herd or pack, it lapses promptly into the wild state; for the spirit of the herd is essentially wild.

Our Western cattle are none of them native. There is no wild native stock except the bison. Our cattle are all European, and represent centuries of careful breeding. I have never tried to trace their several lines back to the aurochs, the European bison—if they can be traced—but the wild blood of that anarch old must have ceased running in their veins long, long ago. Not so his spirit in them. A herd of heavy, bald-faced Herefords, just beneath their corn-fed coats, may be found as wild and dangerous as a herd of these wild buffalo.

We were trailing the "riders" of P Ranch across the plains to a hollow in the hills called the "Troughs," where they were to round up a lot of cattle for a branding. On the way we fell in behind a bunch of some fifty cows and yearlings which one of the riders had picked up, and, while he dashed off across the desert for a "stray," we tenderfeet drove on the herd. It was hot, and the cattle lagged, so we urged them on. All at once I noticed that the whole herd was moving with a swinging, warping gate, with switching tails, and heads thrown round from side to side as if every one of them were watching us. We were not near enough to see their eyes, but the rider, far across the desert, saw the movement and came cutting through the sage, shouting and waving his arm to stop us. We had pushed the driving too hard. Mutiny was spreading among the cattle, already manifest in a sullen, ugly temper that would have brought the herd charging us in another minute, had not the cowboy galloped in between us just as he did—so untamed, unafraid, and instinctively savage is the spirit of the herd.

It is this herd-spirit that the cowboy on his long cross-desert drives to the railroads most fears. The herd is like a crowd, easily led, easily excited, easily stampeded—when it becomes a mob of frenzied beasts, past all control, like the spirit of the city "gang" at riot in the streets.

If one would know how thin is the coat of domestication worn by the tamest of animals, let him ride with the cattle across the rim rock country of southeastern Oregon. No better chance to study the spirit of the herd could possibly be had. And in contrast to the herd, how intelligent, controlled, almost human seems the plainsman's horse!

I share all the tenderfoot's admiration for the cowboy and his "pony." Both of them are necessary in bringing a herd of four thousand cattle through from P Ranch to Winnemucca: and of both is required a degree of daring and endurance, as well as a knowledge of the wild animal mind, that lifts their hard work into the heroic, and makes of every drive a sagebrush epic—so wonderful is the working together of man and horse, the centaur come back! So free and effective the body directed by the human intelligence that fills and rules it like a soul.

From P Ranch to Winnemucca is a seventeen day drive through a desert of rim rock and greasewood and sage, that, under the most favorable of conditions, is beset with difficulty, but which in the dry season, and with the herd even approaching four thousand, becomes an unbroken hazard. More than anything else on such a drive is feared the wild herd spirit, the quick, black temper of the cattle, that, by one sign or another, ever threatens to break the spell of the riders' power and sweep the maddened or terrorized beasts to destruction. The handling of the herd to keep this spirit sleeping is an anxious, and it may be a thrilling, experience.

Some time before my visit to P Ranch in the summer of 1912, the riders had taken out a herd of four thousand steers on what proved to be one of the most difficult drives ever made to Winnemucca. For the first two days on the trail the cattle were strange to each other, having been gathered from widely different grazing grounds—from Double O and the Home Ranch—and were somewhat clannish and restive under the driving. At the beginning of the third day signs of real trouble appeared. A shortage of water and the hot weather together began to tell on the temper of the herd.

It is early in the drive that the wild spirit seems most liable to break out, before the drive has settled to its pace and the cattle grown accustomed to the continuous and insistent authority of the

Cowhands

riders. If they can be carried safely through the first three days, say the cattlemen, there is comparatively little danger after that.

The drive from the P Ranch was started under ill conditions. The first two days were safely passed, but the third day began ominously. The line started forward at dawn, a hot early dawn, and all day long kept moving, with the sun cooking the bitter smell of the sage into the air, and with sixteen thousand hoofs kicking up a still bitter cloud of alkali dust which inflamed eyes and nostrils and coated the very lungs of the cattle. The fierce desert thirst was upon the herd long before it reached the creek where it was to bed for the night. The heat and the dust made slow work of the driving, and it was already late when they reached the watering place, only to find it dry.

This was bad. The men were tired, but the cattle were thirsty, and Wade, the boss of the "buckaroos," pushed the herd on toward the next rim rock, hoping to get down to the plain below before the end of the slow desert twilight. Anything for the night but a dry camp!

They had hardly started on when a whole flank of the herd, suddenly breaking away as if by pre-arrangement, tore off through the brush. The horses were as tired as the men, and, before the chase was over, the twilight was gray in the sage, making it necessary to halt at once and camp where they were. They would have to go without water.

The runaways were brought up and the herd closed in till it formed a circle nearly a mile around. This was as close as it could be drawn, for the cattle would not bed down. They wanted water more than they wanted rest. Their eyes were red, their tongues raspy with thirst. The situation was serious.

But camp was made. Two of the riders were sent back along the trail to bring up the "drags," while Wade, with his other men, circled the uneasy cattle, closing them in, quieting them, and doing everything possible to induce them to bed down.

They were thirsty; and, instead of bedding, the herd began to "growl"—a kind of stifled mutter in the throats of the cattle, low, rumbling, ominous, as when faint thunder rolls behind the hills. Every plainsman fears the growl, for it usually is a prelude to the "milling," as it proved to be now, when the whole vast herd began to stir—slowly, singly at first and without direction, till at length it moved together, round and round, a great compact circle, the multitude of clicking hoofs, of clashing horns and chafing sides sounding not unlike the rushing of rain across a field of corn.

Nothing could be worse for them, for it would only add to their heat and thirst. The cooler twilight was falling, but, mingling with it, rose and thickened and spread the choking dust that soon covered the cattle and shut out all but the dark wall of the herd from sight.

Slowly, evenly, swung the wall, round and round, without a break. I have never seen a milling herd and I can scarcely imagine its suppressed excitement, the waking, the stirring of four thousand wild spirits! To keep this excitement in check was the problem of Wade and his men. And the night had not yet begun.

When the two riders had brought in the drags, and the chuck wagon had lumbered up with supper, Wade set the first watch.

Along with the wagon had come the fresh horses—one of them being Peroxide Jim, a supple, powerful, clean-limbed buckskin, a horse, I think, that has as fine and intelligent an animal face as any creature I ever saw. Wade had been saving this horse for emergency work. And why should he not have been saved fresh for just such a need as this? Are there not superior horses as well as superior men—a Peroxide Jim to complement a Wade?

The horse knew the cattle business and knew his rider perfectly; and though there was nothing like sentiment about the boss of the P Ranch riders, his faith in Peroxide Jim was complete.

The other night horses were saddled and tied to the wheels of the wagon. It was Wade's custom to take his turn with the second watch; but, shifting his saddle to Peroxide Jim when supper was over, he rode out with the four of the first watch, who, more or less evenly spaced, were quietly circling the herd.

The night, for this part of the high desert, was unusually warm. It was close, still, and without a sky. The near, thick darkness blotted out the stars. There is usually a breeze at night over these highest rim rock plains, that no matter how hot the day, crowds the cattle together for warmth. Tonight not a breath stirred the sage as Wade wound in and out among the bushes, the hot dust stinging his eyes and caking rough on his skin.

Round and round rode the riders; round and round moved the weaving, shifting forms of the cattle, out of the dark and into the dark, a gray spectral line like a procession of ghosts, or some morris dance of the desert's sheeted dead. But it was not a line, it was a sea of forms: not a procession, but the even surging of a maelstrom of hoofs a mile around.

Wade galloped out on the plain for a breath of air and a look at the sky. If it would only rain! A quick, cold rain would quiet them; but there was no feel of rain in the darkness, no smell of it on the air; only the powdery taste of the bitter sage.

The desert, where the herd was camped, was one of the highest of a series of tablelands, or benches; it lay as level as a floor, rimmed by sheer rock, from which there was a drop to the bench of sage below. The herd when overtaken by the dusk had been headed for a pass descending to the next lower bench, but was now halted within a mile of the rim rock on the east, where there was a perpendicular fall of about three hundred feet.

It was the last place an experienced plainsman would have chosen for a camp: and every time Wade circled the herd, and came in between the cattle and the rim, he felt the nearness of the precipice.

The darkness helped to bring it near. The height of his horse brought it near—he seemed to look down for his saddle over it, into its dark depths. The herd in its milling was surely warping slowly in the direction of the rim. But this must be all fancy—the trick of the dark and of nerves, if a plainsman has nerves.

At twelve o'clock the first guard came in and woke the second squad. Wade had been in the saddle since dawn, but as this second was his regular watch he stayed in the saddle. More than that, his trained ear had timed the milling hoofs. The movement of the herd had quickened.

If now he could keep them going, and could prevent their taking any sudden fright! They must not stop until they stopped from utter weariness. Safety lay in their continued motion. So the fresh riders flanked them closely, paced them, and urged them quietly on. They must be kept milling and they must be kept from fright.

In the taut silence of the stirless desert night, with the tension of the herd at the snapping point, any quick, unwonted sight or sound would stampede them. The sneezing of a horse, the flare of a match, would be enough to send the whole four thousand headlong—blind, frenzied, trampling—till spent and scattered over the plain.

And so, as he rode, Wade began to sing. The rider ahead of him took up the air and passed it on until, above the stepping stir of the hoofs rose the faint voices of the men, and all the herd was bound about by the slow plaintive measures of some old song. It was not to soothe their savage breasts that the riders sang to the cattle, but rather to preempt the dreaded silence, to relieve the tension, and so to prevent the shock of any sudden startling noise.

So they sang and rode and the night wore on to one o'clock, when Wade, coming up on the rim rock side, felt a cool breeze fan his face, and caught a breath of fresh, moist wind with the taste of water in it.

He checked his horse instantly, listening as the wind swept past him over the cattle. But they must already have smelled it, for they had ceased their milling, the whole herd standing motionless, the indistinct forms close to him in the dark showing their bald faces lifted to drink the sweet wet breath that came over the rim. Then they started on again, but faster, and with a rumbling now from their hoarse throats that tightened Wade's grip on the reins.

That sound seemed to come out of the earth, a low, rumbling mumble, as dark as the night and as wide as the plain, a thick, inarticulate bellow that stood every rider stiff in his stirrups.

But how dark was the night, and how thick the smother of dust! Nothing could be seen; and the hoarse, choking bellow of the head, as thick as the dark and the dust, made all other sounds impossible to hear.

Then the breeze caught the dust and carried it back from the gray-coated, ghostly shapes, and Wade saw that the animals were still moving in a circle. He must keep them going. He touched his horse to ride on with them, when across the black sky flashed a vivid streak of lightning.

There was a snort from the steers, a quick clap of horns and hoofs from far within the herd, a tremor of the plain, a roar, a surging mass—and Wade was riding the flank of a wild stampede. Before him, behind him, beside him, pressing hard upon his horse, galloped the frenzied steers, and beyond them a multitude borne on, and bearing him on, by the heave of the galloping herd.

Wade was riding for his life. He knew it. His horse knew it. He was riding to turn the herd, too, back from the rim, as the horse also knew. The cattle were after water—water-mad—ready to go over the precipice to get it, carrying horse and rider with them. Wade was the only rider between the herd and the rim. It was black as death. He could see nothing in the sage, could scarcely discern the pounding, panting shadows at his side. He knew that he was being borne toward the rim, how fast he could not tell, but he knew by the swish of the brush against his tapaderos and the plunging of the horse that the ground was growing stonier, that they were nearing the rocks.

To outrun the herd was his only chance for life. If he could come up with the leaders he might not only escape, but even stand a chance of heading them off upon the plain and saving the herd. There were cattle still ahead of him; how many, what part of them all, he could not make out in the dark. But the horse knew. The reins hung on his straight neck, where the rider had dropped them, as, yelling and firing over the wild herd, he had given this horse the race to win, to lose.

They were riding the rim. Close on their left bore down the flank of the herd, and on their right, under their very feet, was a precipice, so close that they felt its blackness—its three hundred feet of fall!

Suddenly they veered and went high in the air, as a steer plunged headlong into a draw almost beneath their feet. They cleared the narrow ravine, landed on bare rock and reeled on.

A piercing, half-human bawl of terror told where one of the animals had been crowded over. Would the next leap carry them after him? Then Wade found himself racing neck and neck with a big white steer, which the horse, with marvelous instinct, seemed to pick out from a bunch, and to cling to, forcing him gradually ahead, till, cutting him free from the bunch entirely, he bore him off into the swishing sage.

The steers coming on close behind followed their leader, and in, after them, swung others. The tide was turning from the rim. More and more were veering, and within a short time the whole herd, bearing off from the cliffs, was pounding over the open plains.

Whose race was it? It was Peroxide Jim's, according to Wade, for not by word or by touch of hand or knee had the horse been directed in the run. From the flash of the lightning the horse had taken the bit, had covered an indescribably perilous path at top speed, had outrun the herd and turned it from the edge of the rim rock, without a false step or a tremor of fear.

Bred on the desert, broken at the round-up, trained to think steer as his rider thinks it, the horse knew as swiftly, as clearly as his rider, the work before him. And he knew how to do it, or could see in the dark how to do it, far better than his rider. But that he kept himself from fright, that none of the wild herd madness passed into him, is a thing for great wonder. He was as thirsty as any of the herd; he knew his own peril, perhaps, as none of the herd had ever known anything; and yet, such coolness, courage, wisdom, and power!

Or was it training? More intimate association with the man on his back, and so, a further remove from the wild thing which domestication does not seem to touch? Or was it all suggestion, the superior intelligence above riding, not the flesh, but the spirit?

Chapter X The Rocks
For The Conies

As one of William Finley's first duties as the new State Game Warden of Oregon, he attempted to gather information on the status of the state's wildlife populations—both game species and non-game. He also set about forming a state collection of bird eggs, skins from mammals and birds, and specimens of reptiles and amphibians. He started the collection with his own large one, which he had been building since the early 1890s. Then he hired "collectors" who worked with gun, trap and net. Two of these collectors were Alex Walker of Tillamook and Stanley Jewett of Portland. Both went on to become, after Finley, the best known ornithologists in the Northwest.

After the Finley/Sharp party returned from travels around both Malheur and Klamath marshes, they traveled east, almost over to the Idaho border, into the Wallowa Mountain range. In part, Finley was looking for remaining herds of bighorn sheep, just as he had done in Steens Mountain. By 1912 the animal had nearly been exterminated in the state.

While in the Wallowas, Sharp was very fortunate indeed to be able to see a pika. This interesting high altitude mammal is somewhat secretive, not commonly seen or known to many people even today.

THE ROCKS FOR THE CONIES

We were hunting for mountain sheep in the widest peaks of the Wallowa range, and incidentally had tried fishing in the Imnaha. Such trout! But it is so in all the Oregon rivers. We were after mountain sheep, not trout, and we came off with a cony. It was not the first time. Many an expedition has so turned out; many of mine, I mean, conies for sheep, the feeble folk for the strong rangers of the high hills.

Life is not a matter of size, except, perhaps, to the hunter. To the naturalist and lover of nature, life is a matter of kind, the cony after his kind being as interesting as the wild goat after his kind, or the stork after her kind. I doubt, indeed, if ever the mystery and wonder of animal life impressed me more than while I sat by the cony slide on a peak above the clouds asking the little creature why and why! The geographical distribution of land animals, their successive migrations back and forth between the continents during the geological ages, is a story to stir the slowest imagination; yet no single record of these fossiled wanderings to be read in the rocks ever stirred me more than did the sight of the live cony making a home for himself in the narrow limits of his rock slide in the rifts of the rent and blasted peaks of the Wallowas.

From the gorge of the wild Imnaha we had climbed up and up to the blade-like divide that runs between the head waters of the Big Sheep and Little Sheep Creeks on one side, and the windings of the Imnaha on the other, when our guide and our mammal-collector left us and rode on ahead. They soon struck an old mining trail around the flank of a peak, and, winding about into this, they shortly disappeared. It was near the end of a hard day's travel, and as our indefatigable collector often took such sudden turns, I thought little of it. But that night the two came straggling late into camp with a cony, or "pika," the "little chief," or "crying" hare. This was what they had gone off in such haste for, making a long detour to a certain rock slide on the pass known to our young guide.

The cony is not an animal familiar to many persons. Except naturalists, few climbers who have eyes or ears for so shy, so tiny and rare a creature, and one so difficult to see, ever get into the high altitudes of the cony country. But our guide, who had been a sheep herder and camp tender in the mountains, was an exceptionally keen observer. In crossing this part of the pass the summer before he had heard and seen a peculiar little animal about the size and shape of a guinea-pig among the broken rocks of one of the slides. To this rock slide he had taken the collector, and they had come off with one of the conies, while I, meantime, was trying to keep up with Maud and Barney, the pack mules, descending the other side of the pass, and missing with them an experience that only a few mountain peaks in the world could give me.

I was undone when the two men with the cony came into camp. To have been so near and then, in the company of those clownish mules, to have passed stupidly by! We had descended to Aneroid Lake for camp. Our course from here led down a plunging stairway

Riding into the Wallowa Mountain Range

to Wallowa Lake with never a hope for another cony slide on the trail. We were below the peaks. It was necessary too, that we push forward. Not another day was to be had! Our time was up; and besides, there was nothing left to eat but sour dough bread and condensed milk. This was too true. And my companions imagined that the thought of an extra day on sour dough bread would cure me of my conies. A few days more of it would have cured me of everything. A particularly good fellow was our cook, one of the State's best game wardens; all of which applies only remotely to his bread. It is not necessary for me to live. It is not necessary for anybody to live. But it was necessary for me to see a live cony, though I ate more of Leffel's sour dough bread to pay for it. One may pay too dearly for life. The price on conies, however, is never marked down.

I said nothing that night. Early the next morning one of the men reported the hobbled horses away off in the meadows at the head of the lake; and while they were being rounded up and the kit packed, I left camp unobserved, struck the upward trail and made for the peak of the cony slide.

The sun was high when I found myself slipping and sliding along the sharp slopes in sight of the great rock heap. It was ten o'clock. No wind was moving, no sound or cry of any kind about the slide, no sign of life anywhere.

This must be the place, however. I had passed it at some distance the night before; and here were footprints leading down the bare slope up which I was scrambling. This was the slide, but who would ever have paused here before this heap of broken rock, expecting to see any living thing in it?

The slide was of cracked and splintered chunks that had broken off of the peak above and filled a wash or gully on the side, just as bricks might fall from a chimney and fill the length of a valley on the roof. Stunted trees grew at the base of the slide, and up the side some scraggly grass and a few snow line flowers, squat alpine sorts, blooming bravely along the edge of the melting snow banks.

This was new hunting for me. I crept round the crumbling slope and down to the border of the slide, where I stood trying to make myself believe that animal life of any kind, larger than some of the boreal mice, could climb to this height and here make a home. It was impossible that this barren, blasted pile from the peak could furnish shelter and food enough to keep the fires of any warm blooded life burning throughout a winter! This was the ridge pole of the world. A wilder, barren, more desolate land of crags and peaks could hardly be found.

But here it was they told me they had shot the cony, and had seen at least one other besides it. So I sat down to watch, without faith; for if any creature could live here, what possible reason might there be for his electing to do so.

I was on the roof of creation, looking out and down, the sense of space tingling strangely in my finger tips, the pull of the swinging world as real in my feet as the thrill of the thin air in my lungs. How such attitudes quicken and exaggerate the senses, the nerves and skin, even one's very hairs! I could feel the individual hairs on the back of my hands catch and transmit the message of space, as the wires on the Cape Race Station catch theirs out of the spaces above the sea. As I sat looking out over the wild scene, a great dark hawk wheeled into distant sight toward Eagle Cap Mountain; far below me flapped a band of ravens; and down, down immeasurably far down beneath the ravens, glistened the small winding waters of the Imnaha. But it was the peaks, the scarped, sheer shouldered peaks, stark, black, desolate, standing so close about me, that smote me with awe and a kind of lonely terror. I could stay while the sun was high. How could anything alive stay longer—through a night—through a long winter of nights in this slide on the summit?

For several feet each side of the broken rock grew spears of wiry grass about six inches high, together with a few stunted flowers—pussy's-paws, alpine phlox, beard-tongue, saxifrage, and a low single daisy. Farther down the sides of the ravine crept low, twisted pines—mere mats of trees, prostrate, distorted forms that had clambered and clung in narrow, ascending tongues up and up until they could get no higher hold on the blasted slopes.

And here above the reach of these grim, persistent pines, here in the slide rock where only a few stunted growths and arctic-alpine flowers come into brief bloom through the snow, they had told me lived the cony.

I sat down on the edge of the slide to rest, feeling that I had had my labor for my pains—infinitely more than that, the fierce and fearful glory of the heights—but not a cony. There could be no excuse for life up here. There are living forms in the uttermost depths of the sea, as if thrust down by the weight of water; men in their senses dwell far in the Arctic ice, and even go out into the sagebrush desert to make a home, impelled by I know not what. Strange, unaccountable shifts these, yet not so unaccountable as the choice of such a rock slide as this for a dwelling. For this is the deliberate choice of a race. Only at these heights do the conies dwell, only in such slides of broken rock. As for the stork, the fir trees are her house. The high hills are a refuge for the wild goats; and the rocks for the conies. But this particular slide, while not so lofty as some among the Colorado peaks, was unusually bleak and barren, I am sure. There was almost no fodder in sight, nothing upon which a cony could live long, to say nothing of a colony of conies.

Could this be the place? I must make sure before settling down to the watch, for when in all my days would this chance come again? And how soon would they put a posse on my trail to fetch me back to camp?

Out in the middle of the slide was a pointed pile of rocks with a certain ordered look about them, as if they had been heaped up there by other hands than those that hurled them down from the peak. Going out, I examined them closely and found the bloody print of a little bare paw on the face of one of them. On another rock was the bluish spit of a lead shot. The right place surely. Here they had killed the specimen brought into camp. I went back to my seat content now to watch until they sent for me. The camp must wait on this cony.

I had been watching for perhaps half an hour, when from somewhere, in the rock slide I hoped, though I could not tell, there sounded a shrill, bleating whistle, not unlike that of the mountain ground squirrel's, or the marmot's, yet more tremulous and not so piercing, a trembling, ventriloquial, uncentered sound that I had never heard before.

I held my breath, the better to catch the cry. Again it sounded— up or down, this side or that of the slide, I could not tell. Again and again, plaintive, whimpering, but pure and clear! I gave over my ears and, looking hard at the slide, my eyes fixed nowhere, I watched for motion. Presently, straight in front of me, a little gray form crept over a slab, stopped on all fours, and whistled, waited for a moment listening, then disappeared, The cony!

Gone? I didn't know. I didn't care. I had seen him; and that was almost more than I could believe. The moment was full, and in it the thing was done. What thing, you ask? Why, my becoming a cony, and with him now a dweller in the rock slides of the black and bitter peaks. I have widened my range by that experience, added to my habitat; become one of the Boreal animal forms that push southward on these heights far into my Sonoran zone.

But he had not gone. Keeping as still as the stones, I waited. Presently the plaintive, bleating whistle sounded again from anywhere in the slide. I tried to find the hole into which the cony had disappeared; but the moment my eyes were taken from any spot, it was impossible to pick it out again. The rocks were rough, rusty chunks, two or three feet long, piled helter-skelter without form or order, but with such perfect and confusing repetition of the pattern, that fixed attention at any one crack or slab seemed to set the whole slide in motion. It was like trying to fasten the eye at some fixed spot on the surface of waving water. Add to this the absolute color harmony of the rocks and the cony, together with the creature's polyphonous cry, and you have a case of well-nigh perfect protection. On his slide, even when in motion, he must be almost invisible to the sharpest-eyed eagle.

If you will think of a half grown rabbit, the cottontail, only without a cotton tail, turned into a guinea pig with large, round ears, you will get a pretty fair notion of the size, color, and shape of the cony, perhaps better called "pika," or "whistling hare," or "little chief hare." His legs are all of a length, so that he runs and walks instead of hops; and the soles of his feet are bare. He gets his name "cony" from the cony of the Bible (a very different animal) because, like the Old World cony, he lives among the rocks. The little cony of the Bible is Hyrax, who belongs to the elephant family, a curious remnant of an older time, whose very holding on to life among the rocks speaks well for the protection they offer, scanty as may be the picking about their barren edges.

All the while the tremulous call kept coming from the slide. It was not the cry of several voices, not a colony whistling, as at first I thought, for, however gregarious they may be in a more favorable environment, here I am sure there were very few pairs, if not indeed, a single pair only. There was but one small haycock curing in the stones, and not enough uncut grass in the neighborhood to feed more than a pair of conies for a winter, or so it seemed to me.

As I watched the slide, I finally made out the little whistler, and, with eyes sharpened to their work, was now able to follow him from rock to rock as he moved restlessly about. He called constantly, and as constantly stopped to listen. Plainly it was an answer that he expected. He was calling for some one, and the echo of his own voice disturbed him.

Now he would stop short on a slab and whistle, would lift his head to listen, and, hearing nothing, would dive into some long passage under the rocks to reappear several feet or several yards away. Here he would pause again to listen, then to call, waiting a moment for the answer, before darting into the crack for another search through the tunnels.

Under and over the stones, up and down the slide, now close to me, now on the extreme opposite edge of the pile, he traveled, nervously, anxiously looking for something—for some one, I truly think; and my heart smote me when I thought that it might be for the dead mate whose little bare foot-pad had left the bloody print upon the rocks.

Up and down, in and out, he ran, calling, calling, but getting no answer back. This was the only cony that showed itself, the only live one I have ever seen; but I followed this one with my eye and with the field glasses as it went searching and crying over the steep rock slide until long past noon—with the whole camp down the canon looking for me.

They might have known where to look; out of the canon, back to the roof of the world, to the cony slide—if they could not wait for me.

Higher up than the mountain sheep or the goat can live, where only the burrowing pocket gopher and rare field mice are ever found, dwells the cony. This particular slide was on one of the minor peaks, loftier ones towering all about. Just how much above sea level this one was, I do not know, but far up in the arctic alpine cold in a world of perpetual snow. The conies of Colorado live from ten to fourteen thousand feet above the sea.

By perpetual snow, I mean that the snow banks never melt in the shadowed ravines and on the bare north slopes of the peaks. Here, where I was watching, the rock slide lay open to the sun, the scanty grass was green beyond the gully, and the squat alpine flowers were in bloom, the saxifrage and a solitary aster—April and September together—blossoming in the edges of the snow just as fast as the melting banks allowed them to lift their heads. But any day the wind might come down from the north, keen and thick and white about the summits, and leave the flowers and the cony slide covered deep beneath a drift.

Spring, summer, and autumn are all one season, all crowded together—a kind of seasonal peak piercing for a few short weeks the long bleak, unbroken land of winter here above the world.

But during this brief period the grass grows, and the conies cut and cure it, enough of it to last them from the falling of the September snows until the drifts are once more melted and their rock slide warms in another summer's sun. For the conies do not hibernate. They stay awake down in their catacombs; buried alive in pitch black night with snow twenty-five feet deep above them for nine out of twelve months of the year! Here they are always up on the sides of the wildest summits, living their lives, keeping their houses, rearing their children, visiting back and forth through their subways for all their long winter night, protected by the drifts which lie so deep that they keep out the cold.

Right by me was one of their little haycocks, nearly cured and ready for storing in their barns beneath the rocks; but this would not last long. It was already early August and what haying they had to do must be done quickly or winter would catch them hungry.

They cut and cock the grass about the slide until it is cured; then they carry it all below against the coming of the cold. Naturalists who have observed them describe with what hurry and excitement the colony falls to taking in the hay when bad weather threatens to spoil it.

Hardy little farmers! Feeble little folk, why do you climb for a home with your tiny, bare-soled feet up, up, even above the eyrie of the eagle? Why, bold little people, why not descend to the warm valleys where winter comes indeed, but does not stay? Or farther down, where the grass is green the year around, with never a need to cut and cure a winter's fodder?

I do not know why—nor why upon the tossing waves the little petrel makes her bed; nor why, beneath the waves, "down to the dark, the utter dark," on "the great gray level plains of ooze" the "blind white sea snakes" make their homes, nor why at the north, in the fearful, far off, frozen north, the little lemmings dwell; nor why, nor why—

But as I sat there above the clouds listening to the plaintive, trembling whistle of the little cony, and hoping his mate was not dead, and wondering why he stayed here in the barren peaks and how he fared in the long black winter, I said over and over to myself the lines of Kipling—

> *"And God who clears the grounding berg*
> *And steers the grinding floe,*
> *He hears the cry of the little kit-fox*
> *And the lemming on the snow."*

The Butterflies
Of Mount Hood

As a fitting end to Sharp's summer in Oregon, Finley arranged a climb of Mt. Hood. The climbing party packed Finley's heavy motion picture camera and wooden tripod to the summit. Here he filmed what was probably the first footage from this vantage point. When Sharp returned to Massachusetts, he indeed owed William Finley thanks. As had been promised, Sharp certainly must have had his eyes opened. Today we are fortunate that this summer came about. Sharp's writings and letters give us a valuable insight into regions which Oregonians, along with visitors from other states and countries, view as priceless.

THE BUTTERFLIES OF MOUNT HOOD

How often one becomes the victim of one's special interests! I climbed to the peak of Hood, looked down upon Oregon and into her neighbor States, saw Shasta far off to the south, and Rainier far off to the north, and then descended, thinking and wondering more about a flock of little butterflies that were wavering about the summit than about the overpowering panorama of river and plain and mountain range that had been spread so far beneath me. Or was I the victim, rather, of my inheritance? Was it because I happened to be born, not on a mountain peak eleven thousand two hundred and twenty-five feet above the sea, but in a sandy field at sea level? I was born in a field bordering a meadow whose grasses ran soon into sedges and then into the reeds of a river that flowed into the bay; and I found myself on the summit of Hood dazed and almost incapable of great emotion. So I watched the butterflies.

Or was it that I lacked training? Might one not need to climb Hood many times for the eyes to grow used to seeing and the soul to feeling such unwonted vastness of expanse, such unaccustomed and overwhelming depths? I have tried a hundred times to recall the emotion of my first moment on the summit, and either I had none, or what I had was an utter weariness of body and a depression of spirit due to a sense of my inability to meet the moment emotionally. I felt in spirit as I felt in body, the body perhaps having much to do with the spirit.

We started before seven o'clock from Cloud Cap Inn and reached the summit a little past noon, a steady half day of climb, climb, climb, the last four thousand feet zigzagging across the steep flank of a glacier, the last eighteen hundred feet by the help of a rope from the summit up the sheer ice wall to the peak. I reached the rim of the crater exhausted. Two other strong men of the party came over the rim sick. We had a professional mountain climber with us who was fresh from the Canadian Rockies and who had come to the Rockies directly from the Swiss Alps. He and the guide arrived at the top physically capable of looking at the scene; but the guide did not care to look, climbing Hood being a business with him; and the professional climber (whose business was breaking records) was too disgusted at the wretched time he had made, tied up to us, to look at anything, and was for starting down at once, alone if the guide would let him, to try yet for a record round trip. So here we were undone, indifferent, disgusted, while the kingdoms of this world and the glory of them lay spread out beneath us—and flitting round about us a host of little butterflies.

The day was clear and cool, with a stiff wind blowing across the summit that made our teeth chatter and sent us skulking behind the lumps of slag to get out of its way. Long before we reached the top heavy gaseous fumes began to pour down upon us as the draft drew over the rim of the crater. The wind seemed to clear them from the immediate top, but, looking down into the great pit, we could see a rising cloud of steam that must have carried them in its vaporous folds up out of the heated depths where the ancient fires were still smouldering. Hood is a burned out volcano, as is every cone in the Cascade Range, whose fires were blazing throughout the middle epochs of the Tertiary Period, whose lava flows now spread as sage plains all over eastern Oregon where the stratified ash and tuff lie three to four thousand feet deep. The Oligocene epochs of those flaming fires passed into the Miocene, the Miocene into the Pliocene, when the Tertiary Period gave place to the Quaternary with its Pleistocene epoch of Glacial and Interglacial stages, which, in turn, passed into our present epoch; and still the vapors rise and pour through the rifted rim of the crater down over those glacial snows that lie unmelted on the summit.

The topmost point of Hood is a jagged piece of yellow igneous rock or slag, soft, sulphurous, with the smell of the volcanic fires still strong upon it. Originally a part of the crater wall, it is now but a weathered fragment poised on a pinnacle left by the caving of the rest of the rim into the cavity of the crater. The summit is thus a point, an apex, one of the few high peaks of the world upon which you can stand, and, without moving from your position, box the compass with the landscape, the whole world lying directly beneath you and rounding out to an unbroken horizon that girdles the globe.

And away up here above the world, here over the eternal snows, here in the fumes of old volcanic fires, hovered a host of black and red butterflies. It was an amazing sight. I was prepared for hailstones and coals of fire, for seismic shocks and slides and booming avalanches, but not for butterflies.

Cloud Cap Inn, our starting point that morning, is on the edge of the tree line. We passed immediately into the Alpine zone on leaving the Inn, a few flattened, twisted pines accompanying us for a distance, a few Alpine Arctic flowers going on with us almost to the stony shoulder of Barrett's Spur, some four thousand feet from the summit. But here all life seemed to stop. The Spur rises between the two great glaciers of this side of the mountain, separating them at right angles. It is a high pile of broken rock, so utterly devoid of soil that life could scarcely find a footing here, were it able to climb so high; but the white lupine, the flat pussypaws, the low purple heather, and the purple matted beard tongue could not reach the crest of the Spur. The beard tongue out climbed the others. It was the last living thing that we saw until we reached the summit, except some flies that were sunning themselves at Tieup Rock, nearly a thousand feet above the Spur. The rapid dwarfing of the beard tongue as we ascended was eloquent of the reach and grip of life. When the little clusters or colonies could no longer hold on in the open, they took to hiding behind the pieces of rock, the last of them seeking the shelter of the north sides, where, huddled back from the blight of the noonday sun and the sweep of the blasting winds, they found a slightly moister soil and a temperature a few degrees more equitable, the meager means of a last desperate effort for a highest up. Then the small shadows failed, and we climbed on alone.

It is an impressive thing to leave all life beneath you, to pass from zone to zone witnessing the changes in the forms and the modes of living things as you ascend, but still with life about you, until you find yourself in the presence of an all pervading death. The very sun has changed. You have come within the veil, up through the screen that breaks the fierce light into the prismatic colors of life, and the white rays now blind your eyes and blister the skin of your face and hands. The air is lighter in your lungs; the cold is keen and constant; the look of all things strange and unfriendly.

This leaving of life is so real an experience, as the climber watches the shapeless, diminishing trees, the vanishing ground squirrels, and the last flattened flowers, dwarfed to nothing but root and blossom before they are blotted out, that he can scarcely get up to Barrett's Spur without feeling the presence of death, a consciousness deepened from here on by the extreme narrowness of the footing and the utter withdrawal of space from about him, space that in the crowded valleys of life he had been used to leaning upon.

From the Spur to Tie-up Rock our path was a narrow back that divided the two glaciers. At Tie-up Rock we were belted and fastened together and roped to the guide, who now led us out upon the steep snows that reached up and up to the summit, towering, as it seemed, almost straight overhead.

The climb was without accident, and as mountaineering goes, according to the professional climber, who was last in the string, beautiful enough, but rather tame.

For all of that there was one place in the climb that gave me a shudder, and one moment of thrill, when even the professional climber turned pale. We had ascended perhaps a thousand feet above Tie-up Rock when we came to a crevasse across the glacier. It was a yawning gap, as clean as some awful knife wound through the blue ice, and, illumined by the sunlight, which at that moment shot straight down its unearthly walls, revealed, as not even the heights about us could, the grip of the cold, the depth of the death that lies upon the world. And ten or twelve feet down, taut from solid wall to wall across the crevasse, stretched a stout hemp rope—a human thing frozen into this eternal pit! The sight of it, so unexpected, mysterious, and horribly significant, was shocking. But it proved to be only the rope which the guides had left hanging from the summit the summer before. It had been buried to this depth during the winter, and with slack enough at this place to stretch without snapping when the ice split and the crevasse opened across the glacier.

Working round the crevasse, we kept on till we reached the new rope dropped down to us eighteen hundred feet from the peak. Here we struck our pikes into the snow, breathed ourselves for a minute, and laid hold on the rope. As we did so, a piece of rock, about the size of a large water pail, was dislodged from the summit and started down the sheer slope straight at us. It was dropping down the steps cut by the last climbers to reach the peak, a path as straight to us as the rope could fall. Gripping the rope we swung to one side, watching the wild thing as it came plunging, bounding at us with incredible speed, ready to dodge should it fly at our heads. It was a fearful quarter minute. Down straight at us it tore, struck just in front of us, ripped past with a wicked whiz, hit a hundred feet below us, sprang madly into the air, and, like a bolt, was gone.

Then the real work of the climb began, and to it was added this new alarm of rolling rocks. I had grown by this time quite familiar with the fear of falling, and had ceased to mind it; but I had had no practice in dodging rocks. To be sandbagged on the level is a risk that I have been indifferent to these many years; to be knocked on the head by a ricocheting rock, however, with ten thousand feet to fall, disturbed me considerably. But the guide thought nothing of it. The incident apparently left no impression upon him. He was used to flying rocks. He was used to this particular climb, too. How easily, surely he moved! If I had my life to live over again, I thought, I would be a climber of mountain peaks—so superior did he seem! So admirable is any sort of mastery! And how carefully he moved! Kicking the niche for his toe, or cutting the step into the ice with all deliberateness, giving me time to jack my feet up and fix them where

Sharp on Mt. Hood

his had been. Still the rope that fastened me to him was continually taut; I was loaded with lead. Then the man behind me groaned and stopped. I reached back, took his camera—and it was lead, solid lead. Then the man behind him groaned and stopped, seized with nausea. But the line crawled on up, up, up, through a gateway of snow to the bare rock of the summit.

The experience was worth while; and the view, though too vast, too complete, too sublime for the heart to hold, was worth the climb, and more. I doubt in a few thousand extra feet—the height of

Mount Blanc or Denali—could add anything to the prospect from Hood. The consciousness of such heights might deepen one's sense of awe and terror, but could only blur the earth below and leave one cut off as a thing of clay among the clouds.

So I felt even on the top of Hood until I saw the butterflies. And what a relief, what a surprise to see *Vanessa califorica* flitting about the peak of Hood! I could fallen off for astonishment! I had not seen the butterflies at first. Not until the keen, cutting wind drove us to shelter behind the rocks did I notice the tiny creatures winging past.

We were sitting where we could look into the crater on the one side, and where, directly beneath us, we could see clear down the wall with the rope, to the glacier and the trail over which we had come. At our feet was a small gully, a kind of flue in the crater wall. The draft pulled hard in every direction among the gaps and cuts of the rocks, but hardest up this flue or chimney. The butterflies seemed to be ascending the mountain, coming over the summit by way of the flue, using the draft, as we had used the rope.

But they were not ascending the mountain; they were merely flitting about over the summit, as if the height were home to them. When they had come—how long they had been there—how long they stayed—I should like to know. It was their regular passing at a certain distance from me, and their disappearance in a certain direction, that aroused my curiosity. And the number of them! And that all were coming up, none going down! All of them appearing to shoot up through the little gully or cut between the rocks and to bear off to the right over the crater! What did it mean?

Scrambling to the top of the rock behind which I was resting, and where I could get a survey all around, I saw that the peak was alive with butterflies; that they were flying past my head, and off over the point out of sight around the walls, to reappear far down in the crater, across which they were cutting to my side where, caught in the draft, they were pulled up the flue, up and past my head again, off over the point out of sight to reappear again, far down below, for another turn with their toboggan on the slide of the draft that drew up past us over the summit.

Not all of them were in the game; I caught two as they sunned themselves on the rocks; but that all had played, or would join the fun, and that all had come up for that purpose, I have no doubt.

And what was the game the butterflies were playing over the peak of Hood? And how came they there? And whither went they when the sun sank that night, and the wind swung hard to the north, and the gods of the storms met on the summit?

We saw the clouds gathering below us as we started down. On the glacier walls we met the cold winds climbing up and heard their talk of storm until we came within the shelter of the trees about the Inn. During the night I woke to listen for the sound of feet on the mountain, but none bent the pines outside my window, nor swayed the wide wooded slopes that stretched away to the orchards and the valleys below. Near morning a slow rain began to fall. Was this the talk that we had heard along the heights? This the meeting of those forces flying past us toward the summit? Then through the small stepping of the rain I caught far off a mightier tread, a faint concord of crash and roar—or felt it in the very frame of things, as when an organ fills the deep dim places of the church with trembling, and no note is heard. Hurrying out, I saw the rain slanting down the canon, the dull sky darkening behind the peak, while all about the summit smoked the gray smother of storm. Suddenly the smoke lifted, filled, poured over and down till, caught in some mighty draft, the cloud broke and swept swirling back to the pinnacle in a million flying shreds, where, rounding again into billows, it was torn into streaming sheets that whipped far down the precipitous walls, winding the summit instantly in another shroud of snow.

Gale and snow cloud this morning, where, yesterday, it was butterflies that were playing over the lofty crater of Mount Hood.

Chapter
XII   Mount Hood From
Council Crest

There is one glory of Rainier, and another glory of St. Helen's and another glory of Mount Adams, for these majestic peaks differ from one another in glory, and they all differ in turn from Mount Hood, as Hood, in its difference only, exceeds them all in glory. For pure spirituality, for earth raised incorruptible and clothed upon with the holiness of beauty, Mount Hood, as seen in the heavens from the heights of Portland, is incomparable. Hood is not "The Mountain that was God," but as its snow crowned summit, touched with the warmth of closing day, was first unveiled before me, my soul did magnify the Lord, for the vision, to my unaccustomed eyes, was all divine.

Portland is a city beautiful for situation; Oregon is a State of vast magnificence; and the glory of city and State is Mount Hood. There are loftier mountains—Rainier and Shasta are loftier; there are peaks that fill with awe and that strike with terror, while Hood only fills the soul with exultation, with the joy of beauty, of completeness, and perfection. Hood is but little over eleven thousand feet high, and easily climbed. Its greatness is not physical, not height nor power; but form rather, and spirit, and position. It stands sixty miles from Portland, dominating, but not overwhelming, the landscape, earth and all the sky a frame for it. From Council Crest the city seems a mere spectator looking off at the picture of a mountain rising in majestic symmetry, wrapped with a cold and indescribable purity, yet touched with an aspiration that were fervent were it less profound. Mount Hood from Portland is one of the perfect things of the world.

What will be the influence of this unearthly glory, I wonder, shining down forever upon the city? If there be any virtue, if there be any praise in thinking upon things that are true and pure and lovely, should not the presence of Hood, though acting slowly, act powerfully upon the spirit of the city? Shall Portland be the mother of one great poet, or of one great painter, or one great prophet because, high and lifted up above her streets, stands this holy mountain whose very shape is prophecy, whose radiance is the indwelling light of all true art, and the very soul of song?

Portland is a beautiful city, but born of the river. Young, strong, thriving, she is concerned with sawmills and salmon now, not with the tints on the snows of Hood, though they are often the color of salmon and of richer gold than the heart of pine. Young, eager, adventurous, she is bent on prosperity. Nor does prosperity wait to be won; it comes pouring in upon her, from river and forest and orchard and ranch.

It is hard to think of Portland without feeling the singleness and intensity of her purpose to grow great and rich, as it is hard to write of her without changing from slow footing prose to the gallop of verse. The cities along the Atlantic are full of rich men; but Portland is full of men growing rich. One can sit on Council Crest and see the process, as one can see nothing else, not even Hood, so often is the mountain shrouded in clouds and hid in rain and mist. But where are Portland's poets, her painters and prophets? Asleep in the crater of Hood, I suppose, waiting for the mountain to give them birth.

Portland feels small need of poets now; they are not the stuff of pioneers! How many poets came over the Oregon trail? It seems incredible that the founders of this great city should still walk its streets, should gather in reunion to retell the story of those "early" days of the plains and the Indians, as I saw them gather. The very stumps would still be standing in the streets of Portland had they not been used for paving blocks. Poets are poor hands at pulling stumps and paving streets. And what use has she for painters while her temple walls are rising? Or for prophets when the salmon run their courses up the Columbia as the stars their courses in the skies?

None yet, but the time shall come. The people of Portland are proud of Hood; they are more concerned, however, with their corner lots. The marvel of Portland, according to those who have been there longest, is the rise in land values. There is not a lot in the city but has climbed far higher than the top of Hood. There is magic in Oregon land. The harder you hold it the higher it goes. I should say that the chief activity of the State is holding on to corner lots, a sort of husbandry singularly without virtue here in Massachusetts, but which in

Oregon yields thirty, sixty, and a thousand fold. Towns are being laid out, roads built, farms cleared, orchards planted, and apples, the fairest apples in the world, are being picked, while the tent pins of the population are still unpulled, the people of city and country guarding their land with guns, as it were, or watching their chance to jump some neighbor's claim. The most astonishing thing to me in all of Oregon was the price of land. But then, it is astonishing land. I stopped to watch the plowing of a great field of stubble in Joseph, where, as the plows were turning the black soil around the boundaries, the machines were threshing the yellow grain in the center. The crop had just been cut—sixty bushels to the acre—the stubble being turned in for the next sowing, no manure, no dressing with it to feed the land. And this was the thirty-sixth consecutive year that wheat had been sown in this field, and that wheat had been threshed—sixty bushels to the acre—without a pound of fertilizer given back to the soil.

It is not astonishing that in the middle of such fields the farmers of Oregon are pulling down their barns and building greater in their zeal to make Oregon the biggest barned State of the Union. The heart of the Oregon farmer is in his barn; he has not even tried yet to build for his heart a house.

But this is still true of farmers East as well as West; of merchants East as well as West; as Portland is true of cities East and West. Portland is a typical American city, younger, that is all, and ravishingly fair. Daughter of the river on whose banks she stands, she is the destined bride of the mountain that watches yonder and waits. Hood is in no hurry.

I look down from Council Crest upon the growing city and see the present moment of my country hurried, crowded, headlong—a time of deeds and large and daring conquests, but without sign of "that over-faint quiet which should prepare the house for poets." Then I lift my eyes to Hood, serene and soaring in the far-off Heaven, and lo! A vision of the future! Not the Mountain that was God, but a summit that is song.

Drink, O City of Roses, of the pure cold waters from the snowy heights of Hood. Drink and thirst again. There are other springs in the summit than those which feed Bull Run—fountains higher up of living water such as flowed in Helicon.

The End